CHANGING CULTURES

The Western Isles Today

CHANGING CULTURES

General Editor: Jack Goody

The aim of the series is to show how specific non-industrial societies have developed and changed in response to the conditions of the modern world. Each volume will present a comprehensive analysis, drawing on recent fieldwork, of the contemporary organisation of a particular society, but cast in a dynamic perspective that relates the present both to the past of the society and to the external forces that have impinged upon it. By concentrating on peoples that have been the subjects of earlier studies, some of these volumes will also reflect the developing interests and concerns of the social sciences.

Also in this series

The Nayars Today by Christopher J. Fuller
The Skolt Lapps Today by Tim Ingold
The Yoruba Today by J.S. Eades
Tázlár: a Village in Hungary by C.M. Hann

The Western Isles Today

JUDITH ENNEW

Department of Social Anthropology,
University of Cambridge

CAMBRIDGE UNIVERSITY PRESS

CAMBRIDGE
LONDON   NEW YORK   NEW ROCHELLE
MELBOURNE   SYDNEY

Published by the Press Syndicate of the University of Cambridge
The Pitt Building, Trumpington Street, Cambridge CB2 1RP
32 East 57th Street, New York, NY 10022, USA
296 Beaconsfield Parade, Middle Park, Melbourne 3206, Australia

First published 1980

Printed in Great Britain
at the University Press, Cambridge

Library of Congress Cataloguing in Publication Data
Ennew, Judith, 1944–
The Western Isles today.

(Changing cultures)
Bibliography: p.
Includes index.
1. Hebrides – Social conditions. 2. Ethnology
– Scotland – Hebrides. 3. Hebrides – Social life
and customs. 4. Hebrides – Economic conditions.
I. Title.
HN398.H38E56   309.1'411'7   79-13643
ISBN 0 521 22590 6 hard covers
ISBN 0 521 29572 6 paperback

For my parents, Paul and Edna Morgan

Contents

Illustrations and tables

Tables

Acknowledgements

The research on which this study is based was carried out between 1974 and 1977, supported by a studentship from the Social Science Research Council. At that time I was a research student in the Department of Social Anthropology at Cambridge. Fieldwork was mostly carried out during an extended visit to Lewis and Harris from 1975 to 1976. Short trips were also made in 1974, 1976 and 1977. During the preparation of my thesis and this book I have been stimulated by discussions with colleagues in research seminars in Cambridge, by the unfailing support and advice of my supervisor Dr A. Macfarlane, and by the encouragement of Professor J. Goody. To all of these I extend my thanks.

Every ethnographer owes a debt to the subjects of his or her investigations. To acknowledge individually all the Hebrideans who have given me both hospitality and information would be to produce a seemingly endless list. I hope they will collectively accept my gratitude and forgive any errors in my representation of their social life. Some individuals must be named for the importance of their contributions, for the time and practical help they so generously gave me. Thus I shall take this opportunity to thank Donald Chisholm, Alan and Ann Davidson, Ian Downie, John Dunningham, Robin and Sheena Huggan, Hector and Elsa Ingram, Mea and Alan Jones, Bill Lucas, Kenny and Reeta Macdonald, Norman Macdonald, Murdo Macfarlane, Liz MacIver, Finlay Macleod, Peter and Mairi Macleod, the late Roddie M. Macleod, Murdo Macleod, Victor and Catriona Mackay, Mary Bell and Donald MacSween, Jean Mills, Mr Morrison and the staff of Stornoway Public Library, John Murray, John Paterson and family, Mr and Mrs Roderick and Douglas Taylor.

Additional material and insight on the fieldwork situation was provided by Beverley Brown, Martin Boddy, Charlie Davison, Guy Ennew and Keith Tribe. Keith Tribe also took most of the photographs in this volume and I am grateful to him for permission to use them. Plate 4 is from the Cambridge University Collection and permission to use it was granted by the Cambridge Committee for Aerial Photography. The photograph in Plate 5 was a gift from Murdo Macfarlane to whom I must also express my gratitude for allowing me to quote from his unpublished poem *I saw from me the ben* (p. xiv). In addition I should also like to thank Norman Macdonald for permitting me to use his poem *Strange Meeting* (p. 88), which first appeared in the *West Highland Free Press* in March 1976 and is now reprinted in *Fàd: Poems and Songs in English and Gaelic*, Essprint

Acknowledgements

(1978). In the preparation of the final manuscript Victoria Ebin and Raul Iturra made helpful comments and Paul Beedle gave invaluable editorial assistance.

Prologue

In the autumn of 1977 I visited Murdo Macfarlane, the village bard of Melbost on the Isle of Lewis. Murdo had been one of my chief informants during my extended fieldwork on the island between 1975 and 1976. As is frequently the case in fieldwork, interviews had soon relaxed into conversation, and the subject/observer relationship warmed into friendship. This present visit was a purely social occasion, although the discussion included many details which would inform and enrich my work. Murdo poured me a 'dram' of whisky, while September gales shook the windows and darkened the day into an early twilight. One of the subjects we spoke of was a recent visit by an oral historian. Murdo had been particularly pleased that this observer of Lewis life had questioned him about the labour movement on the island in the 1930s. He contrasted the warm memories he retained of this interview with the visit of another academic, a 'young fool' who 'only wanted to ask about second sight'.

Murdo's obvious scorn of this second visitor confirmed my own perception of writings about the Western Isles. The tendency is to mythologise the islands, to use them to conceptualise notions of Community, peasantry and pre-industrial history. The Hebrides appear to both popular and academic vision as if in a rear-view mirror. They represent the close-knit Community which is apparently lost to industrial, urban existence. Thus they must be seen to be backward, archaic and rustic; an anachronism in the modern world. Outside observers are not usually interested in writing about the way in which the Hebrides are integrated into capitalist Europe. On the contrary, the concern of most students of the area is to construct tradition, to observe old customs and beliefs, to preserve a static picture of culture.

What should be emphasised is the dynamism of the area. This is not the dynamism of hope, for there are considerable economic reasons for describing the islands as depressed. But the Western Isles are not residual. They have moved with the times, albeit awkwardly. Far from being an area untouched by capitalist development, they exhibit in the strongest possible way the results capitalist development has on some areas in every nation state. If the islands were held up in a mirror, the image seen should not be that of a past state in contrast with the present position elsewhere in the United Kingdom. On the contrary, they should appear as the consequence of this present position. This book is an attempt to realise this appearance, to describe the Western Isles as an integral part of the United Kingdom, rather than as an isolated traditional Community.

The dynamic vigour of the Hebridean way of life during my visits in the mid-1970s was characterised by resentment, a feeling of dispossession which contrasted with the warmth of Hebridean hospitality and the wit of much conversation. Underlying all attempts to improve the area is a feeling of insecurity. If Hebrideans are backward-looking, it is perhaps because the future appears uncertain. In the pages which follow I shall attempt to describe the changes taking place in the Hebrides now. These changes do not represent a contrast between tradition and modernity, but are part of a long historical process. The last verse of one of Murdo's poems, *I saw from me the ben*, expresses the occasionally-voiced fear that this process can have only a bitter outcome.

> I saw from me the ben
> A sight that sickened my heart
> Time's dog pursuing my race
> Listen! hear them go down the glen!
> Soon pursuit will be at an end
> The sun sinks in the waves of the West
> Little by little the black night draws tight.
> (Translated from the Gaelic by Norman Macdonald.)

1 The Western Isles 'Community'

The conceptual apparatus of social anthropology has been constructed mainly through the study of non-European tribal and peasant societies. The development of the ethnographic method of British anthropologists took place during fieldwork carried out largely in Africa and Melanesia. With the exception of some important but uncoordinated Community studies like those of Arensberg and Kimball (1940), Frankenberg (1957) and Littlejohn (1963), there have been few attempts to write ethnographies in the British setting. It is no coincidence that these works should be conceptualised as Community studies. The tendency of anthropologists working in European society has been to study rural areas. Consideration of industrial or urban groups is consigned to the realm of sociology. European ethnography seems to be limited to the study of small-scale rural Communities as much like 'primitive' societies as possible. Both the complexities of urban existence and the existence of large resources of historical data apparently overwhelm anthropologists. Boissevain has suggested that they retreat as a result to rural villages, which they study as isolated entities. As far as anthropologists are concerned, Europe has been 'tribalised' (Boissevain, 1975, p. 11).

The notion of Community as an entity is derived from a normative orientation in the work of early sociologists such as Tönnies (1955). He made a distinction between Community and Society. Community is described as the characteristic state of pre-industrial Europe. It is supposedly typified by close-knit, familial, face-to-face relationships. Society, on the other hand, is the outcome of relationships fragmented by advancing industrialisation, with wage labour as the main mode of economic existence. In all concepts of Community there is an implicit criticism of urban, industrial society.

Community studies carried out in Europe have constructed an object based in normative notions and bolstered by assumptions which are taken for granted. They consist of a definable set of texts describing village life in several European nation States, while virtually ignoring the political and economic realities of those states. They tend to assume the existence of contrasts between Community and State, tradition and modernity, rural and urban states of society. In order to isolate the Community as the object of study, they also tend to postulate the existence of mediators or brokers between these contrasted sets (Davis, 1975, pp. 49–50).

Yet the similarities between Community studies should not be taken to

1

indicate a homogenous group of texts. Bell and Newby show in their review of the literature that there are distinct differences in ways of thinking about and studying Communities (Bell & Newby, 1971). They have been described using an organic analogy, as if they were in a state of ecological adaptation and internal equilibrium. They have also been studied as microcosms from which generalisations about macro-sociological processes can be made. Closest to the classical formulations of Tönnies are typological or ideal-typical studies, which place a particular Community at some point along an imaginary continuum. The continuum may stretch from rural to urban, from traditional to modern, from simple to multiplex or between any two poles considered crucial by a particular anthropologist. In all cases the Community is conceptualised as an entity in itself, superordinate to either the people 'in' it or the data 'about' it.

Sometimes Community study is regarded as a form of social research, or methodology. In this case it is dependent upon the inductive method. The object of inquiry is not the Community itself but 'the behaviour of persons' living in it (Arensberg & Kimball, 1940, p. xxv). As Bell and Newby point out, it is not defined in space or time, but is simply a sample which tends to be 'found in small localities studied by face-to-face methods' and not in 'large localities studied by survey methods' (Bell & Newby, 1971, p. 60). This reinforces the apparent necessity for European ethnographers to concentrate on remote rural groups.

These confusions result from trying to demarcate Community as a concrete entity or a representative sample. When Stacey attempted an overview of definitions she pointed out that the feeling of belonging to a particular area is often confused by sociologists with arbitrary delimitations like parish boundaries. She suggests that this is due to a normative orientation (Stacey, 1969, p. 135). But even arbitrary or administrative definitions cannot define Community as distinct from tribal society, even though they may provide an anthropologist with the rationalisation for studying a particular locale.

Arensberg and Kimball's ethnography of County Clare in Ireland is the starting point for British Community studies. It describes several Communities and adopts a culturalist stance. The entity of Community in their book is simply an index of generalised Irish cultural tradition (Arensberg & Kimball, 1940, p. xxiii). This cultural tradition is clearly identical with what the authors conceptualise as social structure. Irish society is described as homogenous and virtually insulated from outside influences. The main components of this society are reciprocal rights, stable population and the 'criss-crossing ties of kinship which are the raw material of community life' (ibid, p. 125). Kin ties are frequently described as if they are the framework of Community life. The family is the archetype of the Community, and its moral form is implicitly what is 'good' in that particular conceptualisation of pre-industrial society.

The classic genre of the European ethnographic monograph is therefore structured around a tradition/modernity dichotomy. In its most distinctive form this can result in an overvaluation of ideas of Community spirit and the family. Thus Franklin's overview of European rural groups implies that there is some unitary form of social structure which characterises European peasantry. As he describes it, social changes in rural areas are changes in this previously static structure (Franklin, 1971, p. 12). This makes it possible for him to suggest that there is a fundamental antagonism between the industrial system and the typical peasant family enterprise (ibid, p. 14).

What is interesting here is that Franklin's notion, of the family enterprise as the unit of production in rural society, gives his concept of Community an economic as well as a moral base. Such an idea could be compared with the work of Chayanov, who based his definition of the peasantry on the idea of the non-exploitative communal relationships existing within family production and consumption units (Chayanov, 1966, p. 125). But Chayanov was writing in the context of Russian post-revolutionary society. He did not visualise the peasantry as a static ahistorical group. It was clear that the post-revolutionary peasantry was the product of recent Russian history, particularly the emancipation of serfs in 1861. The Populist Russian interpretation at the time was that the peasant way of life had been preserved throughout the transition to socialism. But Chayanov appeared to see the peasantry as a specific economic force moving along a path of increased technology, more intensive agriculture and cooperative organisation (Harrison, 1977, p. 324).

Chayanov's work therefore runs counter to the conventional interpretations of European rural life. It is more usual to stress the supposed decay or demoralisation of a synchronic social structure which has been based on family values and Community spirit. It is rare for a European ethnographer to challenge these assumptions in the way that Davis does in his comparative anthropology of Mediterranean societies. He states that 'Mediterranean social order does not . . . refer to an aboriginal society . . . Nor was it ever a complete social order . . . It is rather, those institutions, customs and practices which result from the conversations and commerce of thousands of years . . . ' (Davis, 1977, p. 13).

It is more common for a Community to be studied as isolated from history, as if the entire purpose of the study were accurate description. Emmett's study of a North Wales village shows this tendency (Emmett, 1964). The task she set herself was to form a descriptive analysis of three apparent paradoxes of village life. These were that class distinction did not exist, that poaching was not a response to economic need, and that a high rate of illegitimacy was contrasted with strong chapel disapproval (ibid, pp. xiv—xv). In the construction of her concept of Community she cites the importance of economic factors. These contribute to the stability of family farming enterprises over time, and the extension of kinship ties. Social change in this village is described as merely a residue of the industrial revolution (ibid, p. 131), as if purely material or physical changes, in themselves, promote social change. Thus she writes that 'As transport facilities improve and "village economies" break down, a tendency may be found in many places for people to transfer their allegiance from the village to a wider unit' (ibid, p. 129).

Opposed to this ahistorical technique in European ethnography is the dynamic description of decay. This type of text tends to describe the process of disintegration by comparison with an original state. Notable in this genre is Brody's book on the West of Ireland, *Inishkillane* (Brody, 1974). Brody acknowledges historical change, and contends that the unchanging Irish society described by Arensberg and Kimball is a myth, derived from their functionalist orientation (ibid, pp. 5–6). He writes that 'Arensberg and Kimball have a great deal of data, information and insight about Irish traditional life. They do not seem to have a very developed historical sense: it has largely escaped them that the tradition they discuss was scarcely a hundred years old at the time of their work' (ibid, p. 5). But Brody makes some assumptions of his own about the country people and the 'small communities' in which they live. Indeed he refers to the 'contrast between past coherence and present demoralization' (ibid, p. 17), despite avoiding the error of directly opposing tradition and modernity. It might be suggested that what he described as 'past coherence' amounts to the same Irish myth which he suggests is used by Arensberg and Kimball. Yet it could also be argued that the apparent coherence of the past is a necessary conceptualisation for the people of the West of Ireland. That this is possible will be seen later with respect to the Hebrides (p. 110). The myth of past coherence is an important backdrop to the way in which many Hebrideans conceptualise what they see as present discontinuous change.

Brody admits that the term 'demoralization' is a loosely formulated descriptive category rather than a sociological concept (ibid, p. 16). But this is a less critical theoretical component than the status of the community of Inishkillane, which is an unreal entity, constructed within the text, rather than the description of a real place existing in the West of Ireland. Brody states that 'strictly speaking, Inishkillane does not exist', but adds that 'Unfortunately many hundreds of parishes very much like it do' (ibid, p. xii). Inishkillane is like an ideal type and Brody's description of it takes on the character of an artistic rather than scientific account.

Writing about a Community in its historical setting is one problem. Another is to describe the relationship between a given Community and the wider society of which it is a part. As noted above, Communities are often studied as samples, as microcosms of a nation State, its customs and social relationships. A further strategy is to examine the political integration of a Community into the State via the medium of crucial personae, usually referred to as brokers or middlemen. These descriptions oppose the structure of the Community to the structure of the State, enabling the occupational, ideological, political and communicatory links between the two to be studied. But such an opposition is artificial. The occupants of a rural village do not live in one Community structure and view the State as an externally-opposed structure. They live in and experience both simultaneously (Rosenfeld, 1972, p. 50). As Davis points out, the relationship between Community and nation should not be examined through the study of mediators between two disparate spheres. What is needed is an anthropological consideration of the operations of government and administration, as much as those of villages and peasantry (Davis, 1975, p. 49).

Within Community studies as a whole, the governmental machinery of the nation State is seldom given much consideration. In her study of North Wales, Emmett shows that the members of the Community are aware of, and extremely sensitive to, British society in the form in which it is experienced in the village, 'English landlords own two-thirds of the land in the parish; the quarries which are in neighbouring parishes are owned by English men or companies . . . the English take the place of the upper, upper-middle or ruling class, nationalism being the way through which class antagonisms are expressed' (Emmett, 1964, pp. 4–5). The Community/ State relationship thus appears in an overt political form, as class antagonism between Welsh and English. Similarly, Pitt-Rivers' study of a *pueblo* in Southern Spain implicitly considers the members of this Community as a rural proletariat (Pitt-Rivers, 1954). Yet he describes the peasant's self-conception as a reflection of *pueblo* values, rather than of those of external political groups. The peasant's 'social construction of reality' is visualised as based in the isolated rural Community, even though the actual running of the *pueblo* is the business of outside officials. As Pitt-Rivers describes this Community it is insulated from the external influences which determine many of its rhythms and decisions. It is a portrait of a puppet without strings.

Very few studies show an appreciation of the local significance of national changes. Perhaps the Banbury ethnographies are the sole examples of attempts to examine local politics with respect to national political parties, rather than just in terms of face-to-face power struggles between individuals (Stacey, 1960; Stacey *et al.*, 1975).

All these problems arise because these studies try to conceptualise the reality of a Community from concrete data only. It is not accepted that the data is not *about* a Community, or *derived from* a Community. On the contrary, Community is the logical result of using inductive methods. These considerations have important consequences for a study of the Western Isles. It would not be difficult to describe any one village in the area as a Community. The villages are spatially isolated from each other and each has its own specific characteristics, which are commented on by inhabitants and outsiders alike. Each island in the group likewise has a particular geographical and cultural distinctiveness. Lewis in the north is an area of flat peat moorland, and the people hold strict Protestant beliefs. Barra in the south is a Roman Catholic island, with sandy soil. The inhabitants of Scalpay are known for their fishing skills and prosperity.

The entire string of islands known as the Outer Hebrides or Western Isles is separated from the Inner Hebrides and mainland of Scotland by the Minch. This often hostile channel of stormy sea is thirty miles wide in places, and winter gales frequently isolate the Western Isles from each other and the mainland. There are ample grounds for considering the island group as a Community and examining it in the mode of traditional European Community studies. But as has already been stated, this type of ethnography ignores history and the influence of State apparatuses. If we are going to be able to describe and understand the changing culture of the Western Isles this study must be seen as part of a wider sphere. The islands must be regarded as situated within the historical context of the development and operation of Western capitalism.

Most of the material on which this book is based refers to the island of Lewis. Lewis is the northern part of one island in the Hebrides which is divided into two distinct regions — Lewis and Harris — by a band of rocky, mountainous terrain which still forms an effective barrier to communication. Historically, Lewis and Harris were the territories of distinct clans, and until recently they were administered by the separate local authorities of Ross and Cromarty and Inverness-shire respectively. The islands of North and South Uist, Benbecula and Barra, which lie to the south of Harris, were also once divided into different clan territories (Figure 1). These are the main islands in the group, but there are many more — rocky or fertile, inhabited or uninhabited. Of the many hundreds which can be counted, only thirty are now reported to be populated. One of the most isolated is St Kilda, forty miles to the west of Harris. The present population of this island is reported to be sixty-five. Yet the indigenous St Kildans were evacuated in 1929, at their own request. The new settlers on the island are military personnel, working on a missile-tracking station. As will be seen later, the story of the depopulation and resettlement of St Kilda provides a case study for the rest of the Western Isles. It shows how integration into world economy and a nation State combine to render an environment 'unviable'. It also gives insight into the range of priorities manipulated by central government (Steel, 1975). St Kilda is an image in the rear-view mirror of the Hebrideans which they would surely rather forget.

Although the islands have a varied history of government, they are now a single administrative unit. Since 1974 the Western Isles has been the only political unit in the United Kingdom which is simultaneously a parliamentary constituency and a local authority. Lewis is the largest, and politically and economically the most powerful island. This is partly because Stornoway, the only town in the Hebrides, is situated on Lewis. The town is effectively the administrative centre of the area. It is also the obvious location for new economic enterprises, because of the infrastructure support which it can provide. Thus Lewis possesses powerful psychological advantages.

Because Lewis has been more closely integrated into the economic life of the mainland it could be suggested that it has been subject to more change than the other islands. Certainly Stornoway has most of the amenities one would associate with any small town in the United Kingdom. Compared with the other islands of the Outer Hebrides, Lewis has proved to

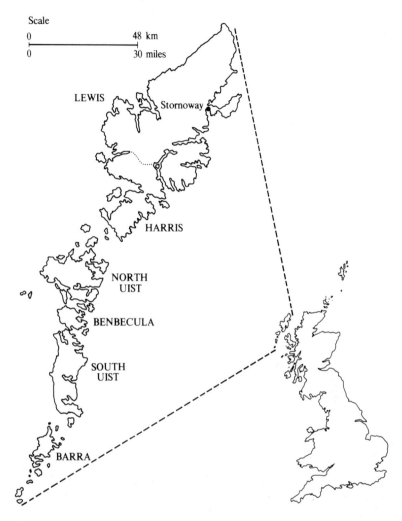

Figure 1. Map of the Western Isles.

have a greater capacity for economic flexibility and adaptation. It is therefore a convenient focus for a study of the changes taking place in the area
as a whole. But most statements made about the rural areas of Lewis are
applicable in a general sense to the other islands. Any significant distinc-
tions, such as those of religious persuasion, will be indicated. But few of
these differences have any noticeable effect upon the overall state of the
Western Isles. The political and economic situation in which the inhabitants find themselves renders them uniformly powerless.

Geographically, the Western Isles are founded on Archaean gneiss, or

7

granite, some of the oldest base rock in Europe. Throughout the islands bare domes and barren ridges of granite dominate the landscape (Plate 1). The rock is heavily scored and worn down by the glacial action of two ice ages, which have also carried away the volcanic deposits which might have provided the basis of a good soil, leaving only a thin scraping of boulder clay. On all the islands there are some peat deposits. Lewis is spread with a blanket of peat, 230 square miles in extent (Plate 2). This varies in depth up to sixteen feet, although it averages five. Peat is the only mineral resource of any consequence, and has been described as 'the Lewis ore' (Hardy, 1919, p. 22). Its main use is as fuel, and continual peat-cutting for this purpose has led to the exposure of potentially arable soil. But extensive rehabilitation of the subsoil has not taken place. This might seem surprising when one compares the Western Isles with areas like the Black Fens of Cambridgeshire where the peat has been reclaimed to form fertile soil. The primary reason is that moorland peat differs considerably from fenland peat. It has accumulated in a wet climate where little evaporation is possible, and from decomposed moss and heather rather than grass and sedge reeds. Moreover, as the islands are based on granite, the peat formed is prone to acidity, which checks the bacterial action necessary for the development of a good soil. Added to this the rainwater which saturates the peat not only fails to neutralise acidity, but also has a leaching effect on any small amounts of alkali present (Astbury, 1958, p. 18).

Despite these difficulties, most of the land which is occupied or cultivated by the inhabitants of the Western Isles has been reclaimed from peat.

Plate 1. Granite boulders scatter the landscape of the island of Scalpay, Harris.

The exception is the *machair* around the coast, where shell-sand has been blown to form a strip of fertile land. This varies from one furlong to two miles wide and is naturally arable. The west coast of the Hebrides from Barra to Harris is relatively well provided with *machair*. Broad beaches exposed to Atlantic winds provide fine shell-sand which is blown inland. The more rocky and indented west coast of Lewis has a narrower band of *machair*. The eastern coasts of all the islands have even less naturally arable land, but are better provided with small, sheltered bays for fishing-boats. The exception is the Point peninsula to the east of Stornoway. This is formed by a belt of sandstone and has deeper, more fertile soil.

Elsewhere, centuries of peat-digging have exposed the boulder clay, and this forms the basis of a reasonable soil when worked with shell-sand and seaweed. This skinned ground, or *gearraidh*, can form good arable soil, but for the most part it is used for rough grazing. Throughout the islands reclamation and cultivation have tended to take place using the traditional *feannagan*, or lazy-beds. These are small, rectangular, ridge-like formations, about ten feet long by four feet wide, which combine the functions of drainage and fertilisation. They are made by spreading shell-sand upon the required area, digging a drainage ditch around it, laying some seaweed over the sand, and then piling the peat or soil on top. This was and is an efficient method of hand-tilling and draining the small, uneven pockets of ground between granite rocks and boulders. There are still very few places in the Hebrides where land is smooth enough for large-scale ploughing or machine-assisted cultivation (Plate 3). The major exceptions are certain areas, prin-

Plate 2. The barren landscape of a Lewis moorland, the geometric lines show the positions of peat cuttings.

Plate 3. A dusting of snow shows up the strip pattern of cultivation of crofts in Tolsta. These crofts have a large proportion of good arable land by Lewis standards.

cipally in Lewis, where peat has been ploughed by the Forestry Commission and coniferous trees have been planted.

These forestry developments are of some significance for the landscape of the Western Isles. The most notable feature of the islands from the visitor's point of view is the almost total lack of trees. In winter this contributes to the bleakness of the environment. The Lewis moorlands in particular stretch endlessly in uniform browns under a heavy and lowering grey sky. In summer, when the moors and hills are gay with heather and wild flowers, the lack of trees to break up the horizon gives an impression of space and freedom.

The other dominant feature is the sea. There are few places in the Hebrides where one is not aware of its presence. The Atlantic breaks incessantly on the western shores, and long sea lochs everywhere penetrate deeply in to the land. Throughout the islands large and small freshwater lochs are spread over moorland and between hillsides, reflecting the ceaseless changes of sky and clouds.

Few settlements besides Stornoway are of any considerable size. Most houses have only a single storey, with perhaps a gable room set into the roof. They are scattered along the narrow roads, and villages are usually separated from each other by tracts of moorland. The houses seem inconsequential compared to the landscape of which they are a part. For the most part the land appears unenclosed. There are few hedges. In some places the land around the villages is divided by low stone walls, but the most usual type of fencing is by post and wire, for which grants are available from the government. This fencing fades inconspicuously into the landscape. Thus, with the exception of the dark slashes caused by peat excavation, the terrain appears largely untouched.

The dominant natural feature of the islands is the weather. The climate is usually described as 'mild temperate' for, although the islands are relatively far north, the shores are washed by the Gulf Stream. But this description gives no indication of the realities of Hebridean weather. The two most noticeable features are wind and rain. In midsummer there are some cloudless, breathless days, when the glare of the sun on the sea dazzles and burns. But there is seldom a day without a sea breeze and the temperature rarely rises to 20 °C (70 °F). Strong winds are common, often rising to gale or even hurricane force. Throughout the year one is conscious of the wind, menacing from the depths of the moorland, wailing across the sea and shaking the doors and windows of houses.

The average annual rainfall of the Western Isles is 40—60 inches. Very little of this falls as snow, for the temperature rarely drops below freezing. The chief characteristic of the weather is its variability. Belts of rain, sleet or hail may be seen racing across the sea or moorland, suddenly blocking out the hills, followed by fitful periods of sunshine, and then again by a further brusque shower. The prevailing atmosphere is damp, and thus, even though the temperature may not be low in winter, one is still aware of the chill, particularly as the wind adds to the general discomfort.

Not only changing weather but also seasonal rhythms play an important part in Hebridean life. The length of daylight varies considerably from summer to winter. In mid-June long evenings linger until close on midnight. If the weather is fine, outdoor activities continue until late in the evening. Agricultural work, fishing and social life bring the people out of their houses, and the pattern of socialising is fluid and relaxed. By mid-December, on the other hand, it often seems as if there is no light until ten or eleven o'clock, and it is dark by the middle of the afternoon. With the days short and the weather inclement, social life alters to a pattern of inter-house visiting. Outside work is cut to a minimum, and only commercial fishing-boats venture on to the hostile seas. Communication with the mainland by plane and ferry is sometimes rendered impossible by rough weather. Summer visitors who are enchanted by the unspoiled beauty of the misty islands would be surprised by the dark forbidding aspect which those same islands show for many of the winter months.

This account of the landscape and climate of the Western Isles must be taken as an ever-present background to the description of social life which follows. The character of the land and the nature of the weather influence many of the patterns of social and economic life which have developed. But it should be remembered that environment is only one influence. Poor resources are often blamed for the depressed economic state of the islands. But the perception of a resource is a social factor. A persistent feature of Hebridean history has been the perception of its resources by external agents. The development of these resources forms the subject matter of the next two chapters.

2 The land belongs to him who works it

It is a cliché in popular literature about the islands that the people there feel a strong attachment to the inhospitable land on which they live. A Gaelic proverb states that 'The bird sings sweetest where it was born', but this does not provide an adequate explanation of the emotional link. Yet unlike many components of the mythologies enshrined in texts on the Hebrides, this feeling is a tangible and influential aspect of social life in the islands. An important aspect of the phenomenon is the concept of ownership which, against much legal and historical evidence, enables the tenants of small crofts to think of the land as their property.

In 1971 the population of the Western Isles was 29,891. The majority of these inhabitants live in crofting settlements which are mostly situated around the perimeter of the islands, within sight of the sea. In the main they do not own the land they work, but hold it from a variety of largely absentee landlords under crofting tenure. This form of tenancy is specific to the Highlands and Islands of Scotland, the seven 'Crofting Counties'. It should not be confused with the Irish system which it only resembles in some respects. Nor should the activity called crofting in Scotland be directly compared with that of Scandinavian countries, where it is a more successful agriculture-based mode of existence.

Crofting settlements, or townships, in the Western Isles appear as straggling lines of houses beside the main roads (Plate 4). A croft is often described as either a 'small piece of land entirely surrounded by legislation', or 'a small piece of land entirely surrounded by advice'. In its basic form it is a patch of land, about one to five acres in extent, on which a crofter has the right to build a house, and for which he pays a low rent fixed by the Land Court. He also has rights in common grazings and peat banks. These rights may or may not be informally shared with other members of the village community who are not defined as crofters. Historically speaking, these other villagers may be cottars, with houses built on crofting infield, or squatters whose homes are built on common grazings. Because of these common rights some crofting agriculture is communally organised, but the extent to which this applies depends upon the population, terrain and history of a particular township. An important aspect of crofting tenure is the extent to which central government intervenes in its administration and regulation through the Crofters' Commission. In the final analysis this body, with its administrative centre in Inverness, can determine which land is designated 'crofting land' and which individuals are designated 'crofters'.

13

Plate 4. The village of Leurbost in Lewis has the typical straggling shape of a Hebridean village.

Crofting as a legally-defined category is less than a century old. Yet it is the crofting way of life which is often assumed to be the basis of the traditional form which is opposed conceptually to modernity. As Hunter points out, crofting is really a transitional state between forms of tribal and private ownership (Hunter, 1976). Land-right problems arose in the deliberate suppression of the clan system by southern government, after the defeat of Highland chiefs at the Battle of Culloden in 1746.

After the 'Forty-Five', a Scottish aristocracy developed on the pattern of the English model. As Youngson indicates, the landholding system of the Highlands prior to the Act of Union in 1707 was tribal rather than feudal (Youngson, 1973, p. 11). Lowland Scotland was subject to a feudal polity, but the rule of Scottish kings was not effective in the rough terrain of the Highlands and Islands until the eighteenth century. In these remote and wild parts of Scotland the clan was the unit of military and social organisation. In early times, according to some writers, the system was a form of democracy. The chiefs were chiefs for life only, and were raised to this position through election (Seebohm, 1883, 1971; Mackenzie, 1903). As the chief was a military leader he counted his wealth, not in land or produce, but in the number of men he could muster for battle. Thus, although the clan resembled a family unit in ideological terms, the actual genealogical connections between the followers and their chief might be of adoption rather than blood. When Samuel Johnson visited the Highlands in the eighteenth century he referred to patriarchalism and paternalism. He stated that the Laird's power was strengthened by consanguinity, which produced kindness from the Laird and reverence for patriarchal authority. 'The Laird was the father of the Clan, and his tenants commonly bore his name' (Johnson, 1775, p. 135).

The internal structure of the clan in early times is a matter of dispute, but it is clear that the introduction of hereditary chiefships encroached on what was originally a more communal form of landholding. In the original trusteeship, an elected chief held the land in trust for followers who had common rights of usufruct. The land was inalienable from the common body of the clan. But hereditary lines developed. The overlordship of particular families became acknowledged, and was ratified by the production of bardic poetry. Each chief held court with a resident official bard, who would have a kinship connection with the privileged lineages. Likewise, the bardic circuit of travelling Gaelic poets spread political influence. The staple verse of this period 'recounts genealogy and history (either factual or fictitious) and praises both the quick and the dead' (Thomson, 1974, p. 23).

The Act anent Lands Lying Runrig, passed by the Scottish Parliament in 1695 brought tenurial practice to this hierarchical system. The Act broke up common landholding practices and increased inequality in the possession of clan land. It created what amounted to a new class of middlemen or tacksmen. A tacksman held a part of the clan land, or 'tack', from the chief and sublet it to other tenants. The original qualification for tackholding was close relationship to a chief. During the eighteenth century when the Highlands and Islands were opened up to southern travellers, tacksmen were frequently blamed for the poverty-stricken state of their subtenants. On Lewis, however, the tradition is that the tacksmen 'imported useful knowledge of agricultural methods and treated their subtenants sympathetically' (Lewis Association, Report No. 7, p. 7). These were most probably hereditary lines of tacksmen who claimed propinquity to the island's laird. Twenty-two holders of the sixty-four larger tacks on the 1718 Rent Roll bore the name of the laird, Mackenzie. But this does not necessarily indicate local sympathies. The traditional Macleod chiefship of Lewis was usurped by the mainland clan of Mackenzie in the seventeenth century.

A further group of tacksmen held their land on commercial leases, rather than inheriting a tenancy for which they paid in actual or potential military service. It is this group which is often blamed for conditions of hardship among subtenants, who had no security of tenure, and from whom high rents were extracted in cash, kind and labour. Subtenants were tenants-at-will until the Crofting Act of 1886. Rent arrears were common and complaints about rising rents and evictions can be traced back to the middle of the eighteenth century.

15

An additional element in tenurial change was that after the 1745 Rebellion the prestige of a Highland chief no longer lay in military power. He had to maintain a status position in the manner of the English aristocracy. Rents were increasingly demanded in cash rather than goods or labour. The tacksman class became more commercial, occasionally being replaced by professional farmers. Frequently, chiefs decided to dispense altogether with the intermediate class of tacksmen and collect their rents directly. On Lewis the status of tacksman was abolished in the early nineteenth century when the impoverished laird decided to take direct control of the estate and run it with the help of a chamberlain and factors.

Communal ownership of the land by the people who work it is therefore not a feature of island history in the modern period. Even during the medieval period it is likely that the institution of hereditary chiefship had already eroded common rights of alienation and usufruct. Tenure rather than ownership has been the landholding system for most of the inhabitants of the Western Isles for at least three centuries. The patriarchal relationship of laird and follower was long ago replaced by that of landlord and tenant, as money rent and the farming potential of land became more important than the military following it could support. In some areas of the Highlands and Islands tacksmen emigrated in large numbers, and subtenants became farm labourers for professional farmers (Collier, 1953, pp. 43–4). In the Outer Hebrides communal farming practices were altered in favour of a system whereby the grazing land was still held in common although each family had the allotment of a separate arable plot. The crofting townships thus formed were often the result of a number of families being moved from fertile land to make way for sheep-farms. The formation of sheep-farms in areas which had previously been characterised by mixed farming on smallholdings was one means by which landlords could increase the income from their estates.

Older people in the Western Isles can remember the tales of evictions narrated by their parents. They re-tell the stories with conviction and in great detail. One inhabitant of Brue, on the west side of Lewis, recalls his family saga by beginning: 'When my people were evicted my grandfather was sent from his own house in Galson, which he had built thirteen years before. He got no compensation. They had five of a family, and my grandmother had to carry on her back my father at the age of two, a distance of eight miles.'

This family, like twenty others, had been evicted from the village of Galson which the landlord planned to be part of a sheep-farm. This proprietor, Sir James Matheson, was a new type of laird for the Islands. The Seaforth family, a branch of the mainland Mackenzie clan, had been forced to sell their Lewis estate in 1844 because they were deeply in debt. Matheson was a wealthy Scottish merchant, who had made a fortune in trade with the Far East. He had many plans for the improvement of the island and brought about extensive changes.

Four of the families evicted from Galson went to Brue in the year 1863.

Significantly, none of these four had large rent arrears, although some others from Galson had arrears abated and their passage to America paid by Matheson. The crofts in Brue to which the Galson families moved had just been vacated by tenants who travelled in the same vessel across the Atlantic. The passage money for these tenants and their families was £121; the arrears abated totalled £3.18s 3d according to the factor's entry in the Rent Rolls. But the rent of the South Galson farm rose between 1869 and 1889 from £67 to £436 a year. The resentment felt by Lewis people against these wholesale evictions was shown in their behaviour towards the tenant of the farm. J.P. Helm is remembered by reputation as 'a wicked rascal'. The Stornoway Sheriff's Court imposed a constant stream of fines and short prison sentences against crofters from the area who allowed their sheep, cattle and horses to roam over his land, who cut turf and heather on the farm, and who repeatedly removed gates and fences. On one occasion, in December 1893, while Helm and his shepherds were in Stornoway in connection with one of these interdicts, forty-three of his young male sheep were mutilated. No culprit was ever apprehended for this symbolic act.

The four families from Galson had been moved to crofts on a part of Brue known as 'Brue-New-Lands'. The soil had only recently been broken in by families who had been moved, as one descendant puts it, 'from the rich lands of Uig' further south. At the other end of the village, nearer the sea on the sparse but more fertile *machair*, were twelve crofts of older standing. It is recalled that there was constant friction between the inhabitants of the two parts of the village, but neither had been there for long. The location of the village is artificial, not based on a rational use of natural resources. The soil of Brue is some of the poorest in Lewis; the common grazing had to be taken from the neighbouring village of Barvas.

Claims to autochthonous rights in the land by the present generation are thus not founded either in communal ownership ratified by ancient law, or in continuity of occupancy. The legal statuses of 'croft' and 'crofter' were only established through the Crofting Act of 1886. The 'traditional' crofting way of life is therefore less than a century old. The shifting existence of the crofting population before the Act is evident in the Rent Rolls for the Parish of Barvas. These indicate that the case of Brue is not untypical. It was not common for one family of crofters to have been living on the same smallholding for generations. The rotating system of agriculture known as 'runrig' was still in use in Lewis in the early nineteenth century. The Reverend James Headrick complained about the inefficiency of this method in a report to the Mackenzie family (Headrick, 1800)' 'Runrig' would have favoured attachment to the land on the basis of clan rather than family membership.

It was not until the 1820s and 1840s that crofts became marked out in anything like their present form. From the Rent Rolls of 1851–99 it is clear that lots were often exchanged between unrelated individuals, within or between villages, sometimes through a cash transaction. Successive chamberlains, factors and ground officers seem to have manipulated some of these transactions in order to redress arrears and balance the estate accounts. Sometimes a crofter in deep arrears had his tenancy terminated in favour of a newcomer who paid all or part of his predecessor's debt. Occasionally a factor noted that the incoming tenant had paid for the house and contents, while the previous tenant moved to wage labour in Stornoway. Sometimes the old tenant might be given his passage money to emigrate, although this usually happened when large numbers were evicted, and bore no relation to arrears. Sometimes the outgoing tenant remained on the lot. A note by the factor in the Rent Rolls would then state that the previous tenant lived as 'a pauper in a bothy', while the new tenant had given an undertaking to support him in his lifetime.

In Brue, under a systematic re-allotment of land, the crofts became regularised into their present format of twenty-eight. The method by which this took place shows that even the estate factors had to acknowledge some kinship rights in the land. Young couples who had been unable to obtain a croft frequently settled in a separate house built on the croft land of a parent. The new household often obtained an unofficial share in the lot, usually a quarter or a third, occasionally as much as one-half. In the reallotment of 1880 these shares were regularised and the numbers reallocated. Thus William Matheson was the original crofter on Number 3 Brue, paying a rent of £2 7s. His son-in-law, Norman Paterson, had a separate house on Number 3 with one-third of the arable land. When the crofts were reallocated Norman retained his third of the land, paying £1. 1s rent and becoming the new Number 3 Brue, while William paid £1. 7s rent on a reduced croft renumbered 4 Brue.

The forms of succession usually practised were inheritance by a widow, son or son-in-law. Widows now seem to have first claim on the croft, but some Hebrideans claim that this was not the case formerly. There is a tradition that mothers were often turned off the croft by a son, and that it was only after the 1886 Act that their inheritance was secured. There is no evidence of this in the Barvas Rent Rolls, however. Where a son inherited he was not always the first-born. Although male succession seems to have been the overall preference it often took the form of ultimogeniture or inheritance by the last-born. This is often still the case because older sons may have emigrated or found crofts of their own. The claim of a son-in-law on a family croft operates through a daughter who has probably remained in the family home. This claim may be valid even if there are living, older sons. It is the child who remains in the family home and works the croft who in practice becomes the crofting tenant, both before and after the 1886 Act. This happens even if there are two houses built on the same croft. It is the sibling who lives in the family *home* who tends eventually to inherit.

The ideology, however, is of primogeniture and agnatic inheritance. These principles show in bequests made after 1886. Wills are usually made in favour of the eldest son, who, more often than not, does not live on the croft. He may have been living in Australia or Canada for many years. In some cases he will no longer be in communication with his family. Crofting legislation requires that he is contacted so that he can claim the croft or sign it over to another member of the family. Where the family has lost contact with the heir this process can take several years. In the early years of the Act this often meant that remaining individuals in the family could be *de facto* tenants, paying the rent and working the croft, but they could not become *de jure* tenants until the legal claimant had stated his preference. Crofts can thus be legally untenanted for ten or twenty years, and complications can arise if the *de facto* crofter dies before the legal claimant is found.

The Crofting Act of 1886 was a crucial factor in determining the pattern of present landholding practices. To some extent it relieved the problems experienced by the inhabitants of the Highlands and Islands. It fixed the croft as an heritable subject, set fair rents and allowed compensation for improvements to be paid by the landlord when a tenant quit a croft. But agitation over land rights continued for forty years after the Act. The feeling of being deprived of rightful possession of the land is still strong in Highland folk-memory. The privations of the nineteenth century are kept alive in the tales of older people and in popular histories.

The usual chronicles of the history of Lewis tend to narrate changes in ownership of the island as if they were merely the result of family feuding or accidents of history. But the motivation behind these changes can be shown to be largely economic, and this was the cause of the distress and misery experienced by the islanders.

In the seventeenth century the people of Lewis had a change of laird. The main influence behind this was external to the island and related to the way in which its natural resources were viewed by outside agents. For nearly four centuries the island had been held by the Macleods of Lewis, known as *Siol Torquil*, or Torquil's seed. By the seventeenth century this hereditary lineage was weak, and the island riven with internecine disturbance. The Scottish Crown was threatened by an alliance between the Western Isles and Ireland, and merchant interests in the South were becoming interested in the potential wealth of the Minch fisheries.

In 1597 an attempt was made to establish royal political and economic control in the Highland regions. An Act passed by the Scottish Parliament in the same year provided for the establishment of three Royal Burghs in the area. The foundation of burghs as trading centres was the means by which feudal society controlled the Lowlands. James VI used the Confederation of Burghs to help maintain order in his kingdom. The merchants of these communities had a vested interest in keeping the peace between feuding factions in Scottish life, for this encouraged trade and increased their prosperity (Smout, 1969, pp. 27–8).

Of all the areas in King James's kingdom, the most lawless was considered to be the Western Isles. The King was anxious to impose peace and a measure of respect for government, and to do this he used a shrewd mixture of force and colonisation, and enlisted the support of powerful Highland chieftains. Only one Royal Burgh was actually set up in the Highlands, but a Council of Ten was appointed to advise the King on the establishment of more. Official ideology was that law and religion should be brought to the islands, but underlying this was the need to replenish the royal exchequer (Gregory, 1836, pp. 277, 287). Some members of the Council also came to have a personal, financial interest in the improvement of the islands. By an Act of 1598, Lewis, Harris, the lands of Dunvegan and Glenelg were put at the King's disposal. The island of Lewis, and part of Skye, were then granted to a company of Lowlanders, at least one member of which was also a member of the Council of Ten. The Lowland company was then allocated further land in Skye and Harris. This created a potentially powerful island party which threatened the interests of at least one mainland chieftain, Mackenzie of Kintail.

The party which eventually went to colonise Lewis is usually known as the Fife Adventurers. They were under the overall command of the King's cousin, the Duke of Lennox, and consisted of a party of impecunious gentlemen, volunteers and mercenaries, together with 500—600 hired soldiers. The terms of their commission when they arrived in Lewis in October 1599 were to establish the rule of King and Kirk. The adventurers settled around Stornoway, where they built a 'pretty town', after overcoming the initial resistance of the Macleods (ibid, p. 290; Mackenzie, 1919, p. 60). But cold, disease and a lack of proper shelter, together with the difficulties of getting supplies, worked against them. Only a precarious existence was maintained by means of an uneasy alliance with Neill Macleod, one of the two surviving bastard sons of Ruari Macleod who had been the last undisputed lord of Lewis.

The King's plans to pacify the islands himself were delayed by his accession to the English throne in 1603. The adventurers were forced to leave after an attack by Tormod, Ruari's legitimate son, who had previously been in the custody of Mackenzie of Kintail. Five years later a more determined band of colonists forced Tormod to yield and deported him to Edinburgh. But they were still faced with hostilities from Neill. The King granted the island to a further set of colonists who attempted to invade the island in 1609. But Kintail had arranged for Neill Macleod to seize their supply vessel. The shrewd mainland chief had also sent his brother to 'aid' the colonists. Faced with this duplicity and lacking supplies the colonists disbanded their forces and sold their title to Kintail. Mackenzie then obtained a commission of 'fire and sword' against what were now described as 'rebel' Lewismen, and in 1610 he overran the island (Gregory, 1836, pp. 334—6).

This series of events reveals more than a simple tale of Highland feuding. It shows two new elements entering island existence; the urge of Lowland Scotland to exploit Lewis's resources and a change in ownership which was as much economic as it was political. As Smout states, King James's pacifying efforts did not bring peace to the Highlands, but they 'drove home

the lesson that those chiefs who were to prosper were those who were prepared to back their King, and to keep good lawyers in Edinburgh as well as
sharp swords at home' (Smout, 1969, p. 105).

The Minch fisheries attracted further interest in subsequent decades,
but they were exploited principally by mainland, southern or European
vessels. Native Highlanders and Hebrideans lacked the capital to invest in
larger boats which could compete with these foreign interests. The
Mackenzie family, soon to be invested as Earls of Seaforth, made attempts
to improve local fishing operations. But their main exploitation of island
resources was in the manufacture of kelp, and this directly affected the
pattern of island landholding.

Kelp is a collective name for a variety of seaweed and is also the term
used to describe the ashes of these seaweeds when burnt. The calcined
ashes yield alkalis, which were used extensively in the eighteenth century
in the manufacture of soap, glass and alum. To engage in kelp manufacture
was therefore to be involved in producing raw materials for southern industrial enterprise. Hebridean kelp production appears to have begun in the
mid-nineteenth century. The seaweed was cut by subtenants using sickles
and piled into kilns on the beaches. The kelp was liquefied, being stirred
all the time with irons, and then left to cool and harden. Finally it was
covered with turfs until a ship came to collect it for the market. The work
went on day and night. A visitor to the islands at the time commented that

This is the hardest labour which the people have throughout the year and
at the time they are worst fed; because their own potatoes or little grain
are by this time mostly consumed. The oat meal . . . is very sparingly dealt
among the people that if possible, they may not eat more of it than the
price given them for making each ton of kelp can afford. And thus, instead
of paying their rents with the summer's labour they may sink deeper into
their master's debt (Buchannan, 1793, p. 159).

Thus, although wage labour of a kind had entered the Hebridean economy,
it was likely to be commuted to a form of indebtedness, which operated
through the medium of rent on land.

At the peak of kelp production, Lewis alone produced about 700 tons a
year (Gray, 1957, p. 127). The beaches yielded a plentiful supply of seaweed, and subtenants provided a large, captive, labour force. At the beginning of the nineteenth century the Napoleonic Wars prevented the import
of foreign alkaline substitutes for kelp, so profits to the landlords were high.

The subtenants suffered from two disadvantages. They could not par-
ticipate in the market without the aid of the landlord who alone could provide transport, and they were thus obliged to sell to him at whatever price
he chose to fix. Second, although the raw material was free-growing, it
was subject to the legal monopoly of the proprietor. Because tenancy was
not legally regulated, the landlord was able to manipulate tenancies on
agricultural land in order to produce the labour force required for kelp
production. The tenant did not have free access to raw materials except

through the landlord, and was therefore obliged to labour for piece wages. Rents were increased in order to force tenants to do this (ibid, pp. 129–31). The profits gained by the landlord were seldom spent improving the estate, but were required to keep pace with the English aristocracy in the southern court. As the kelp season coincided with the growing and fishing seasons, agriculture was neglected and fishing declined. No new skills were learned from kelp manufacture, which required only manpower. This requirement led to a subdivision of agricultural holdings in order to support a larger labour force, and the period of comparative prosperity resulted in a rising population. Between 1755 and 1801 the population of the Outer Hebrides increased by 139 per cent (Collier, 1953, p. 172).

After the Napoleonic Wars the southern market for kelp collapsed because imports of cheaper substitutes were available. Highland landlords protested when import taxes were reduced, but to no avail. Despite the high profits gained in kelp many landlords were already in debt, and Seaforth was one of the most impecunious of these lairds. The fall in kelp prices occurred at the same time as a reduction in cattle prices. Cattle had for centuries been the mainstay of the Highland economy. In trade with the south it had been a vital form of currency (Gray, 1957, p. 42). With the loss of this important source of income both laird and tenants were forced further into debt.

Seaforth's reaction was to try to increase rentals yet again. But the overcrowded population on his Lewis estate was underemployed now that large-scale kelp production no longer took place. The tenants could neither pay cash rents nor procure the means of subsistence from their meagre holdings. Seaforth therefore tried to improve the agricultural value of his land by initiating large-scale sheep-farming. Highland prices were rising because sheep-farms could be let to wealthy tenants. But for this to be possible the people had first to be cleared from the land. This was the motivation behind the evictions and forced emigrations referred to above. The laird's problems were not solved by this means and the Seaforth family was obliged to sell the Lewis estate to Matheson in 1844. The change of ownership did not reduce the tenants' difficulties. The records of the nineteenth-century Rent Rolls bear witness to the source of those feelings of dispossession which are still experienced today.

The problems of tenants did not go entirely unremarked in the south. The national politics of the British State in the nineteenth century recognised a 'Hebridean problem'. An intervention of the State in the affairs of the Highlands and Islands was judged to be necessary when the failure of the potato crops in 1836 and 1837 increased the sufferings of the people. Official policy at the time favoured emigration. The overcrowded Highlanders were described as a 'redundant population'. The provision of State aid to famine-stricken areas was not regarded as a suitable remedy, for poverty was regarded as a personal failure of the poor. The 1834 Poor Law Amendment Act discouraged State aid, which was believed to encourage the inherent laziness of the unemployed or destitute. Estimates of the total number of people to be removed from the Highlands made by the Select Committee on Emigration of 1841 encompassed about one-third of the total population. In evidence to the Committee it was stated that special magazines were being circulated among Highlanders to 'instruct the people on the subject of emigration' (Select Committee, 1841, pp. 62, 82).

Thomas Knox, who was the Chamberlain of Lewis, stated to the Committee that tenants on the island were not entirely destitute. He estimated that 400–600 bolls of meal would be needed for relief in 1842, and that 600–700 inhabitants should be forced to emigrate. It is doubtful that this would have relieved congestion or destitution on the island. Knox suggested that land released by eviction and emigration should be kept as sheep-grazings and not reallocated to the remaining tenants. He also expressed the opinion that 'a great deal might be done in shifting them from one part of the island to another' (ibid, pp. 170–81).

Because of the constant shiftings and uprootings of the population it was difficult for tenants to combine their forces and protest in an effective manner. It was not until much later in the nineteenth century, after crofting land had been formally reallocated, that political agitation for land reform took place. Southern newspapers began to devote space to accounts both of evictions and of land raids which illegally marked out crofts on sheep-farms formed by evictions (Kellas, 1966, p. 9). In 1882, after an incident in Skye known as the Battle of the Braes, Gladstone's Liberal government was forced to declare a state of emergency in the Highlands. In Glasgow, Edinburgh and London the forces of Highland, Irish and Liberal interests began to combine to fight for land-law reform. This culminated in the formation of the Highland Land League in the 1880s. The League has been described as the first successful labour movement in Britain. Although it was originally organised in towns, it rapidly formed branches throughout the Highlands among crofters and by 1884 had a fully paid-up membership of 5,000 (Hunter, 1974a, p. 52).

At its first annual conference at Dingwall, the League presented a manifesto proposing revolutionary changes in rights of landed property. It also announced its intention of supporting candidates who favoured these proposals at the next election. The Franchise Act of 1884 allowed crofters the vote for the first time, and the League successfully harnessed the militancy of the Highland region. Five 'Crofter MPs' entered Parliament.

As a result of the League's political action, the Napier Commission had been formed in 1882 to investigate conditions in the Highlands and Islands; following this the Crofting Act was passed in 1886. The body of the Napier Report was concerned with definitional problems, with sorting out mythical from legal land claims, and real from imagined grievances. It also attempted for the first time to define crofting tenure. Despite socialist agitation for nationalisation of land, the Report only sought to apply remedial action to the existing landholding structure. Although it paved the way for legislation which offered some degree of security for the crofter, it did not propose any radical restructuring of tenurial practice. It has therefore been credited with creating a 'rigidity in the crofting structure which is the cause of many of its difficulties today' (Taylor Report, 1954, p. 13).

As far as the inhabitants of the Western Isles were concerned, the main fault of the 1886 Act was that it failed to return their appropriated land. A leader in the *Lewisman* of 1889 claimed:

We cannot be responsible for
  WHAT THE FOLKS ARE SAYING
That the crofters are surely satisfied with the rents now fixed.
That they are really not much better off than before.
That what is wanted is more land at the rate fixed by the Commission.
That there is not a Crofter in Lochs will pay a penny of the Arrears or rent
  fixed by the Commission until the squatters are removed from their lots.
That the agitation is only at the commencement.
That there is no destitution now, but that there is worse, there is famine.
That the Lochs people say they cannot live through another winter unless
  they have another raid.

These raids were organised by the Land League as a form of protest in which the landless and dispossessed returned to areas from which people had been cleared, and staked out holdings for themselves. In many cases the occupation was largely symbolic. The biggest protest on Lewis was the Park Deer Raid of 1887. This had been secretly organised for months. Huge numbers of Lewismen marched into the Park deer forests in the Lochs district and stayed for two nights, killing a reported 200 deer. The deer were roasted and eaten amid scenes resembling a religious festival, and indeed members of the Free Church were prominent in the Land League. The press and other visitors were invited to the feast to listen to the crofters' grievances and to hear 'the causes which induced them to resort to this method of hunting for food' (Macdonald, 1967, p. 203). The event resulted in a successful defence of the raiders in an Edinburgh court. But the Park land was not returned to the people, and it remains to this day a sporting estate.

Land raids continued sporadically until the First World War. Constant demands were made for large sheep-farms and sporting estates to be broken up into crofts for the overcrowded and underemployed Lewis people. Bitter disappointment was expressed because it was felt that government promises to share out large estates had been broken. There is much justification in these complaints. Although a Commission of 1892 scheduled 1,782,000 acres of Highland arable and pasture land as suitable for small-holdings, only about 23 per cent was actually used (Taylor Report, 1954, p. 16).

The inhabitants of Lewis suffered appalling losses in the First World War. These were magnified by a tragic shipwreck in which many of the returning survivors were drowned within sight of Stornoway. During the war the island was purchased from the Matheson family by Lord Leverhulme, and it was to him that the disappointed and embittered islanders turned with renewed demands for land. The interchange between the anti-socialist, capitalist autocrat and his insistent tenants became a national issue, and the matter was settled partly by State intervention.

Leverhulme bought the islands of Lewis and Harris late in his career. By the time he became the proprietor he was a well-established businessman, with a worldwide network of companies. The foundation of his fortune had been soap manufacture, and he was well known as the founder of Port Sunlight in Lancashire, a town built to house his employees. The resources of the Lever Brothers group of companies and his global interests, together with a considerable private fortune, undoubtedly helped Leverhulme to view the Hebridean problems of distance from market and lack of capital as capable of solution. He had wide-ranging plans for the development of the resources of Lewis. He decided that the future prosperity of the island should be founded on the 'harvest from the sea'. Harbour facilities were refurbished and generous loans made to local fishermen on advantageous terms. The transport and marketing problems were tackled simultaneously. Plans for a canning factory were made. Market outlets were set up throughout the United Kingdom by the formation of a new company, MacFisheries.

Leverhulme's plans were a conspicuous failure and some versions of the story imply that peasant resistance to modernity was the cause. One writer lays the blame on 'Lewis Independence' and a refusal to perform wage labour (Murray, 1966, p. 184). Some local people express the opinion that Leverhulme's plans were 'ahead of their time'. But the plans failed mainly because of a mixture of old land-right problems and external economic factors.

The new proprietor's sole condition for the implementation of his enterprises was that some crofters who combined agriculture with a little fishing should become full-time fishermen (Nicolson, 1960, p. 36). He had commissioned an economic survey of the island's resources. The conclusion of the report stated that 'No land used as land is used in Lewis will pay . . . [you should] specialise and separate the crofter and fisherman. Either can be made profitable if well understood. Both lead to double failure when combined' (Hardy, 1919, p. 124). It seemed self-evident to Leverhulme that the fisherman-farmer could not generate a viable income. He suggested that the full-time fishermen should have only small plots of land on which they could grow vegetables for their own use. This amounted to a refusal to break up the much-resented large farms into crofting holdings. But many of those who returned from the First World War still claimed that the farm land had been wrongfully taken from their forefathers. They now demanded that farms should be reconverted into crofts, convinced that they had a right to land which they had defended with their lives (Nicolson, 1960, p. 47). It was only a subsidiary appeal to tradition which stated that the islanders preferred the economic pluralism of fishing and farming, in which each man had independent control over his time and labour. A large proportion of the population already had experience of wage labour with mainland fishing operations. Unfortunately for Leverhulme the Scottish Secretary of State, Robert Munro, chose to support the crofters, largely on the grounds that the government had a commitment to return the land to crofters.

Although the Highland Land League had now fallen into disarray, land reform had become a concern of both the Scottish labour and nationalist movements (Crowley, 1956, p. 125). When Lewis crofters began a new wave of land raids in the 1920s they received the support of left-wing organisations on the mainland. John Maclean, the Communist leader, made a visit to the island and claimed that land raids were the rural equivalent of industrial strikes. He saw the problems of Clydeside and the Highlands as part of the same 'general crisis of capitalism' (Hunter, 1975, p. 201). These Lewis land raids were not symbolic like the Park Deer Raid. Farms at Gress, Tong and Back were invaded and crofts staked out. At Gress the crofts on the old dairy farm remain now in the pattern marked out over fifty years ago. The inhabitants of this part of the village maintain a superior attitude to those in the other part of Gress, whose plots were legally allocated some time later.

But Leverhulme's plans did not fail simply because the State intervened to ratify the crofters' illegal action. Between 1920 and 1921 it became obvious that he had also overstretched his resources elsewhere. Through an unwise purchase of a company in Nigeria, Lever Brothers became liable for debts of £2 million over and above the £8 million purchase price. Banks and underwriters were unhelpful, and Leverhulme himself was pressed for arrears of supertax (Nicolson, 1960, p. 165). Within a few years of his purchase of the islands Leverhulme, now an old and sick man, was forced to abandon his plans and sell his Hebridean estates. In an extraordinary gesture Leverhulme tried to give the land to the crofters, with the exception of any who had taken part in raids. But apart from a few individual 'free gifters' and the town and parish of Stornoway, which is now managed by an elected body called the Stornoway Trust, the crofters refused the offer. The rest of the island is now owned by either small private landlords and companies, or the Department of Agriculture and Fisheries for Scotland.

Three considerations arise from this account of land rights on Lewis. First, the claim to ancient ownership of land on the island is not based on rights of usufruct which stretch back over centuries. Few, if any, of the crofters could substantiate a claim to till land originally worked by their distant ancestors. Likewise, crofting in its present form is a relatively recent form of tenure. Communal land ownership may have existed in the time of clan ownership, but alienatory rights were vested in chiefs by the sixteenth century, if not earlier. Secondly, land agitation in the nineteenth century appears to have been more concerned to establish tenurial rights than rights of absolute ownership. The Highland Land League differed from its Irish counterpart in this respect. While the Irish call was for nationalisation of land, the rank and file of the Highland League were more interested in fixing tenurial practices. When Leverhulme offered the land as absolute property to crofters, even those who accepted showed some reluctance. One reason given was that acceptance would make them liable for the owner's share of local authority rates, in addition to the proportion they already paid as tenants. Thus, although feelings of dispossession are frequently expressed by islanders, the act of repossession, even in land raids, may only go so far as establishing tenurial rights. Finally, many of the changes in outright ownership of the islands have been caused by the acts of outside bodies. As the Western Isles have gradually been brought under the control of central government so the ownership of the land, the pattern of its exploitation and the exploitation of its inhabitants have changed over the centuries.

3 The 'traditional' economy and its transformation

Changes in land ownership in the Western Isles have affected the recent development of economic life. But at no time in recorded history have the islanders been wholly self-sufficient in agricultural produce. Export of cattle provided one earlier source of income. Fishing activities also provided food and other important products. Earlier this century, crofts were intensively worked and crofting townships supplied many of their own needs. Each croft was worked as a family unit, although the infield was not always fenced off into individual plots, and there was a good deal of co-operation between families.

The house and a small garden for crops such as kale would be enclosed by a stone wall. Besides this, the only means of enclosure would have been a stone dyke round the village which separated arable infield from rough grazing. Within the dyke all was 'black ground', used for growing essential crops for the inhabitants and their stock. The animals kept at this time were mostly cattle and horses with some poultry. There would have been relatively few sheep as these were mostly the stock of commercial farmers.

Under the Crofting Act of 1886 each crofter had a right to the arable infield around his house, and to a share in the common grazings of his village, including the peat-banks. In the pattern of rural life which the elderly now remember from their childhood, activities varied with the seasons. But it was not simply changes in the weather and the length of day which determined the rhythm of existence. As rents had to be paid in cash and many essential items purchased from outside the village, there was a need for some members of each family to perform wage labour. A principal source of cash income was fishing. The Minch herring fisheries were exploited largely by foreign interests. Large boats financed by mainland and European capital followed the migrating herring in their seasonal journeys around the British coast.

Herring stocks are found when the fish are either feeding or spawning. The latter provides the best catch as the fish are well-fed and in good condition. Spawning grounds are situated seasonally at different points in the North Sea or North Atlantic. From December to February the shoals are found around Iceland or off Western Norway. In February and March they migrate to the Shetlands, the Minch, Northern Ireland and Ayrshire. In spring and early summer the fish travel to the North Sea, and by June and July they are found again off the Shetlands, in the Minch and around the Isle of Man. For the rest of the summer months and into early winter the North Sea once more provides the best herring-fishing grounds (Hodgson, 1957, pp. 16–19).

In the nineteenth and early twentieth centuries it was by following the foreign vessels which pursued these fisheries that cash income was brought to the Hebrides through wage labour. Men contracted to work as deckhands during the season. They did not confine their labour to the time when the fishing-fleet was concentrated at Stornoway but followed the herring to the Shetlands, Ireland and the coast of East Anglia. Other men were employed on the quays as coopers, making barrels for the cured herring and supervising curing operations. But for Hebridean folk-memory the most significant group of wage-earners from the fishing industry were the 'herring girls'. Young Hebridean women were employed as gutters and packers on the quays when the fleet was operating from local harbours. Many unmarried girls followed the fleet as it pursued the migrating fish.

In early May, fish-curers, or coopers acting as their agents, would go to the villages to recruit girls in teams of three. The curer gave an advance of money, called in Gaelic *an aileas*, which amounted to a contract of service. This meant that the girls had agreed to go away for the season to towns like Lerwick or Fraserburgh, Aberdeen or Great Yarmouth. Special boats, and even trains, were used to transport the girls to foreign ports. On arrival they often had to go straight to the quays to begin work. The hours of standing, working with hands covered in brine, often stretched from dawn to dusk. The lodgings were sparsely furnished. Frequently landladies cleared the rooms of furniture and carpets, leaving only wooden boxes as seats. In the Shetlands the girls slept in dormitory huts. The low rate of pay often left them in debt for their passage home. During this migration their belongings were packed in wooden trunks or 'kists', in which they would also store small gifts as surprises for the family back home. Many of these 'girls' still live in the islands. They are elderly now, but their experiences have acquired a symbolic function in the formation of the Hebridean self-image. They epitomise the importance of fishing; the necessity to migrate, even temporarily, to obtain a cash income; the alternation of poverty and gaity; the love of and return to the Home (Plate 5).

With active men and young women away during the busiest agricultural months of the year, the burden of cultivation fell upon wives, children and the elderly left behind. They would be fully occupied tilling the ground around the village with spades and occasionally horse-drawn ploughs. The main crops were oats, barley and potatoes. One of the heaviest tasks was cutting peats for fuel. Hebridean fishermen repeatedly tried to have a closed season declared on Minch fishing in the spring, so that they would have time to help with this essential work. Villages had their own kilns for drying corn, and in many places there were watermills for producing flour. Cattle were kept for milk, butter and cheese. While crops were growing close to the village the animals were grazed away on the common pasture. Some people stayed overnight with the cattle in shelters known as 'shielings'. Many returned to the village on foot early in the morning, carrying

Plate 5. Herring girls and coopers from Lewis at the turn of the century.

the milk, and remained during the day to help with agriculture or peat-cutting.

During the summer months there was plenty of fresh herring to eat, but in Lewis this was often bought from Stornoway. Villagers who did not catch their own herring purchased barrels of ready-salted fish for winter use. Many rural families had their own small boats but fishing was usually line-fishing with whiting, ling and cod as the main catches. People cured their own fish for the winter, either by salting or drying, and fish-oil was saved for a multitude of purposes. It was an intensive existence which did not cease in the long winter months. Then the family became home-centred and was engaged in practical indoor activities. These included spinning wool, weaving tweeds and blankets and knitting other garments.

It is often suggested that crofting and fishing, with the addition of weaving, provide the ideal existence for the inhabitants of this area, each occupation fitting the other in a rhythmic yearly cycle. But, as has already been shown, commercial fishing operations removed the more active members of the family group when their labour was most needed. Originally, weaving operations took place in the winter months. The cloth was only produced for local consumption. But in the early part of the twentieth century, government attempts to improve conditions in the Highlands and Islands included plans to increase weaving activities and produce cloth for external markets. In Lewis this has resulted in the growth of the Harris Tweed industry. Originally, tweed production was spread throughout the Western Isles, but it has gradually become concentrated in Lewis. The comparative prosperity of Lewis, particularly Stornoway, has thus tended to increase at the expense of less well-favoured areas of the Hebrides.

The position is analogous to the relationship between the Western Isles and the rest of the United Kingdom. Because the economy of the islands cannot be regarded as self-sufficient or autonomous, it is necessary to examine the economic situation as part of the development of capitalism in the United Kingdom and the rest of Europe. Just as the landholding system cannot be thought of as a traditional static form, so the economic life of the islands has to be described in dynamic terms.

The economic situation of marginal areas like the Hebrides tends to be viewed through the perspective of regional economics, which relies on an implicit division between traditional and modern systems within a nation State. The field of regional studies has arisen within the discipline of economics alongside the growth of the governmental or public sector in market economies. It is concerned with the observation that, where State economies are planned, policies which are successful at a national level may not be so satisfactory at a regional level (Johnston, 1971, p. 20). Although regional economics lacks any well-defined or universally agreed principles it is centred on the idea of economic growth, which has been the cohesive concept in economics for three decades (ibid, p. 26). Regional economics delineates special regions by reason of their cultural homogeneity and relationship to the core of the nation State. Spatially remote regions, such as the Highlands and Islands are thought of as lagging behind the dynamic core of growth because of natural disadvantages. It is claimed that progress towards the fully developed condition of the core can only be achieved through permanent subsidy from the nation's prosperous heartlands (Jones, 1974, p. 569). The problem is usually described in terms of a high level of unemployment experienced in the region, and the ideal solution is usually the provision of employment in industrial production. Thus it becomes easy to conceptualise the 'marginal region' as pre-industrial, and it is easy to set up a contrast between its 'tradition' and the 'modernity' of other regions.

In studying an area like the Western Isles in detail it becomes evident that such a contrast is not viable. The elements which are said to be part of a static tradition are often discovered to be relatively recent. In many cases they have evolved through the effects of an industrial or capitalist development which may be either internal or external to the area. Such was the case with the effects of kelp production upon the tenurial practices of the Hebrides. A similar reason for changes in landholding was the development of capitalist-oriented methods of sheep-farming. Comparable histories are found in fishing and weaving, the 'traditional bases' of Hebridean economic life.

During the nineteenth century, Stornoway harbour became a busy centre for fishing-vessels. Other harbours in the Hebrides like Tarbert, Scalpay, Eriskay and Castlebay also took part in the Minch fisheries. At the height of the season the quays were busy with gutting, curing and

31

kippering operations. Elderly people recall that it was sometimes possible to walk across the harbours over the decks of the boats moored there. The herring fisheries were controlled by foreign curers who hired areas on the quays, known as 'stances', during the season. It was these curers who provided wage labour opportunities. The markets they supplied with cured herring reached far into Northern Europe.

Local curers controlled the white fisheries in a smaller scale of operations. The Napier Commission Report stated that island-based curers of cod and ling 'kept shops in which they sell clothing, boots and shoes, fishing-gear, pots and pans, groceries, provisions etc' (Napier Report, 1884, p. 176). Under the system in use at the time a boat was supplied to a crew on credit. Food was also provided to the crew and their families and a balance was struck at the end of the season against the fish caught. The price paid for fish would have been fixed at the beginning of the season. According to the Sheriff Substitute for Stornoway, who reported to the Commission, the prices charged to indebted fishermen were higher than normal. He mentioned the case of a boll of meal costing £1 to an ordinary customer which might be £1. 4s on credit to a fisherman. He added that the risk of non-payment was very great and that the curer's capital might be hopelessly sunk in crews. 'In the vast majority of cases, the crews are in a state of chronic indebtedness, and fish for him, year after year, with little prospect of being free' (ibid).

It is not clear from the Napier Report if debts such as these were incurred by the crew as a unit or by individual members. The evidence of the Rev. W.A. Smith, writing in 1875 about the west side of Lewis, indicates that boats were purchased initially by curers and that each crew member paid one share in an individual contract with the curer. Smith estimated that the average debt for a crew of eight would be £100. He noted that competition between curers meant that men could move freely from one to another, so that debts could be regarded as fictitious. He added that fishermen, knowing they were being overcharged for provisions and gear, had no intention of discharging their debts and might deposit money in the bank rather than repay the curer (Smith, 1875, pp. 40—4).

Many of these smaller curers were simply merchants and chandlers. Others had wider commercial interests, like the emerging tweed industry. One local fish-curer estimated that the number of local curers in Stornoway rose from six to fifty between 1853 and 1887 (Cottar Report, 1888, p. 35). One claim is that curing interests were encouraged by the payment of bounty money from the government for fitting-out fishing-boats. The bounty money paid to curers could be used by them as advances to fishermen in order to tie them for the following season (Thomson, 1849, pp. 83—4).

The fish-curer's role gradually changed from middleman to initiator and entrepreneur. In the late nineteenth century fish-curers were a respected class of businessmen, frequently based in Stornoway. Their diversified interests included salvage, shipbuilding, shipowning, banking, tweed merchandising and general commerce. One curer, Aeneas Mackenzie, was described as the 'head centre of Lewis Toryism' (*Highland News*, 2 December 1893). He was a frequent speaker at public meetings and prominent in the Temperance Society. His wife was also an important figure in Stornoway society. Among his business interests he was a shipowner and salvage contractor, and he advanced credit to smaller curers.

In the 1880s market-price fluctuations and the removal of the bounty caused liquidity problems for many curers. They began to abandon the custom of tying boats to fish for them and replaced the seasonal arrangements of fixed price with a daily auction of fish, by which they could pass on market fluctuations to the fishermen. At the same time credit on provisions and gear became difficult to obtain as the curer's direct interest in keeping the boats at sea began to wane.

The bulk of fishermen at this time appear to have been landless cottars. These were people who had built a second house on a family croft. They fished with lines from small boats and their meagre catches compared unfavourably in size with those obtained by the trawlers and steam-drifters increasingly used by mainland fishermen. The credit supplied by curers had formerly lasted their families through the summer. Now they were faced with destitution as soon as their potato supplies from the previous year ran out in the spring. A report on the cottar population of Lewis prepared in 1888 found that the people had no money, could not obtain credit and were forced to kill their stock for food. They were in a state of 'the deepest poverty and dejection' (Cottar Report, 1888, p. 5).

As a result of this distress, direct loans had become available from the government. These supplied up to three-quarters of the price of a boat and two-thirds of the cost of gear. In 1887, £8,716 was lent to eighty-nine Highland fishermen. A further 111 applicants for loans were unable to raise the 25 per cent deposit. Even many of those who were considered creditworthy were in debt two years later, and large arrears were eventually written off as irrecoverable. The Lewis record was somewhat better than the rest of the Highlands and Islands. In 1902 the Lewis balance sheet for money loaned on ninety-three boats showed that thirty-five had been redeemed in full, fifty-two had been given up and only sixteen were still in debt. Lewis fishermen had repaid 82.4 per cent of the loans. Other crofting areas as a whole had only repaid 59.5 per cent.

Thus the state had begun to take the place of the curers in the provision of credit. Fishermen could sell their catch on the open market. But this was the basic failure of the loans scheme. The grants were too small to purchase boats which could be used competitively in an open market. Moreover, because Hebridean fishermen were dependent to some extent on the produce of their crofts, they preferred to fish from their home ports. But these small harbours could not in most cases support larger vessels. Grants for boats needed to be supplemented by grants for the provision of better harbour facilities. The Hebridean fishermen were caught in a cycle of inferiority (Gray, 1972, p. 106). They were reported to be using only a 'perfunctory method' with few boats at sea, and no systematic fishing.

Even where, as at Stornoway and at Castlebay, the herring fishing was at its height there were comparatively few local boats engaged in it; those that were not employed, we were told there as elsewhere, were being 'got ready' for a fishery which only lasts for eight or ten weeks, and which was already considerably advanced (Walpole Report, 1890, p. 7).

The next decisive factor in the decline of local fishing operations was the First World War, which took away most of the active men. Boats were tied up for its duration. After the heavy losses of wartime, when those who had survived returned, they discovered that the boats were no longer serviceable. In addition, the Eastern European market for cured fish, which was the mainstay of the Hebridean export trade, was on the decline (Lewis Association, Report No. 5, pp. 10—14). This was partly because of changing tastes, but also because the Baltic countries were building their own fishing-fleets and becoming independent of imports. Leverhulme's plans for the local fleet failed, although the marketing outlet of MacFisheries continued to expand as part of Lever Brothers' enterprise.

Between 1920 and 1924 there was a massive exodus from the islands as able-bodied men, who might have built up a new fleet of small boats, emigrated to the colonies. A few of those who remained managed to band together. They became tied to local merchants in the steam-drifter network. But most of the boats landing fish at Stornoway during the boom in Minch fisheries in the late 1920s were from foreign ports. The main income from fishing was once again derived from wage labour. The 1930s saw a decrease in fishing. This was partly due to the general recession, but mostly because of a slump in Scottish fisheries. This was the result of the government sanctioning the import of cheap Norwegian herring (ibid, p. 12). In 1935, under the Herring Industry Act, there was a reorganisation of the industry. Loans were made available for boats and gear, and an authorised export scheme was established. The home market expanded, particularly during the Second World War. But for the islanders these benefits were short-lived.

After the war Stornoway was built into the major fishing port of the North Minch, with extensive improvements to the harbour. This further influenced the concentration of industry and amenities in Lewis and away from the other islands. The Herring Industry Board established a meal- and oil-reduction factory, a kippering plant, and quick-freezing and cold-storage facilities. But in the same period the local fleet declined. By 1959 there were only twenty-five boats larger than forty feet long registered in Hebridean ports, and only six full-time crews in Lewis (Blake, 1964, p. 115). Loans for boats were available from government agencies, but most people could not raise the necessary deposit. Commercial fishing operations were confined mainly to Stornoway, Scalpay and Eriskay, while small boats were used in each village to catch fish for home consumption. The small size of the fleet, together with a high rate of outmigration, meant that in many places the father—son tradition, through which fishing knowl-edge could be passed on, was at an end. Even those who still retained con-fidence in fishing as an occupation lacked experience of modern equipment and techniques.

In the 1970s fishing and fish-processing provides work for about 6 per cent of the employed population. The days when Stornoway quays were thronged with herring girls and coopers, working through the long summer days, are over. Stornoway is still an important fishing port. There is a local fleet based there, as there is at Scalpay and Eriskay, although the fishermen from these two islands land their catches either at Stornoway or on the mainland. The new fishing-fleet is composed of men who regard themselves as full-time fishermen. It has been established relatively recently and has only a contingent relationship to traditional Hebridean fisheries.

Some of the incentive for recommencing the fishing industry came from local enterprise. In Scalpay, for instance, the efforts of one family which had accumulated capital in cargo-boats, were sufficient for fishing oper-ations to begin again. The small but miraculously sheltered harbour is now home port for a successful small fleet which has grown up with the help of government loans and grants. Scalpay fishermen are famous throughout the Hebrides for their prosperity and their willingness to accept innovation. In Lewis it was recognised that the requirements for rebuilding the fleet were new boats and trained men. The Herring Industry Board had already gone a long way towards providing commercial inducements to land at the home port. But the provision of boats required capital, and some scheme of education was needed to train men to become fishermen.

Capital became available in 1959 from the Macaulay (Rhodesia) Trust which had been established by a wealthy expatriate to benefit his home-land. The trustees announced that they would provide the deposits for local men to purchase boats under the scheme operated by either the Herring Industry Board or the White Fish Authority (Blake, 1964, p. 116). The men had to be full-time fishermen, either trained in modern methods or willing to be trained, and they had to give an undertaking to remain in the industry. At the same time the government decided to sponsor a similar type of scheme from the resources of the Highland Fund. The project began in 1960 under the title of the Outer Hebrides Fisheries Training Scheme. Despite some unexpected financial setbacks, the target of twelve new boats was reached. These were nearly all equipped for dual-purpose fishing, making all-year-round work possible. About sixty local men were trained, most of whom were previously employed in the merchant navy, whaling, weaving or mainland fishing (ibid, p. 121). The extent to which the tra-dition of fishing had broken down prior to the initiation of this scheme can be judged from the comment of the fishery officer in charge to the effect that many of the men had to be taught to mend nets.

After the success of this scheme, the Highlands and Islands Develop-ment Board, which was set up in 1965, started another along the same lines. It also made an investment in fish-processing and boatbuilding. There has therefore been an increase in outlets in Stornoway for the catch. All catches landed have to pass through the North Minch Fish Selling Company, which acts as a buffer between the shore and catching industries. This organisation's main role is to auction the fish, but it has subsidiary roles as banker carrying the debts for running costs, and as accountant looking after the paperwork and records of individual vessels.

The boats usually leave their home harbour on Monday, provisioned for a week, and fish the waters of the Minch. Locally-owned boats are too small for the Atlantic. They are equipped to fish pelagic fish like herring and mackerel as well as white fish, shell-fish and lobsters. The gear includes expensive, usually hired, electronic devices for locating shoals. Although the catch is varied, Hebridean fishermen tend to regard themselves as herring fishermen. The migratory and fickle herring is a fish which has to be energetically pursued, and these fishermen implicitly regard themselves as hunters, despite the sophistication of their equipment.

At the end of each week Stornoway inner harbour is packed with small vessels, many of them local. The quays are busy with fishermen mending nets and maintaining other gear (Plates 6 and 7). The offices of the North Minch Fish Selling Company and the fishery department of the Department of Agriculture and Fisheries are perpetually busy. There is an easy, gossipy atmosphere. Both fishermen and officials have a single deep concern, the fish. But despite the informality of proceedings there is no doubt that this is a professional, commercial venture. Hebridean fishing is a business activity.

Plate 6. Fishermen on the quay of Stornoway inner harbour

The mortgages on the eight Lewis boats purchased under the Outer Hebrides Fisheries Training Scheme were paid off well within the twenty-year loan period. The Highlands and Islands Development Board loans scheme has not been quite so successful, but there had only been one fore-closure at the time of fieldwork. Some second-hand boats purchased under a more recent scheme have been paid for in full. The Stornoway-based fleet is increasing in size, skills and capital assets. Twenty-five locally-owned boats were operating from the harbour in 1976, with owners and crews drawn from all over the island. At least two of these vessels were being purchased through banks rather than government-sponsored schemes. The result is a new breed of professional fishermen, who regard crofter-fishermen with some scorn, describing them as 'anglers'.

Despite these developments, the problem of under-capitalisation remains. The rich fishing grounds of the Minch continue to be exploited by larger foreign boats, and local boats remain too small to venture far into the North Atlantic. In 1976 the Highlands and Islands Development Board financed exploratory fishing of the areas of the Atlantic to the west of the Hebrides which were already exploited by boats from Spain, Holland, France, Russia and even Japan. They discovered that, among the stocks hitherto unused by British fishermen, those of the blue whiting merited further attention. There are processing problems associated with this fish, which deteriorates quickly and has a lower-than-average food yield. Yet it is the prospect of large catches from the North Atlantic which has

Plate 7. The main shopping street in Stornoway overlooks fishing boats in the inner harbour.

prompted the building of new pier and harbour facilities and a processing factory at Breasclete on the west coast of Lewis. Some disappointment was felt in Barra that the factory was situated in Lewis. It is estimated that the plant will employ thirty-four people, and this would have eased the unemployment situation in Barra. Moreover, the Highlands and Islands Development Board is confident that Breasclete will develop into an important fishing centre on the strength of the North Atlantic fisheries.

For local fishermen the prospects are not entirely promising. Because the Minch had been overfished by outside interests a ban on herring fishing was imposed in 1978. If it continues, this will have disastrous effects for islands like Eriskay and Scalpay which are almost entirely dependent upon herring fisheries, although mackerel still provide an alternative catch. The main difficulty is that Hebridean boats remain too small to take advantage of the potential of blue-whiting fishery. Despite the multi-million pound development at Breasclete, it seems that foreign boats will continue to dominate the exploitation of resources in the waters surrounding the Western Isles. Some local fishermen report difficulties in attracting loans for larger competitive boats from the Highlands and Islands Development Board. Only one large second-hand boat has been purchased by a local contractor and his family. There are promises of finance for further vessels but the future of Hebridean local fishing cannot be said to be completely hopeful.

The history of these fishing operations is one in which external agencies have dominated the exploitation of local resources. In the case of the Harris Tweed industry the story is that of a local development which was progressively protected from outside competition by legislation. The evolution and structure of this industry demonstrates the futility of analysing the present Hebridean situation in terms of a tradition versus modernity model.

Harris Tweed is represented in the media and in advertising material as a traditional textile. The *Harris Tweed Handbook*, for instance, refers to the production of tweed as a combination of natural environment and traditional skills. It claims that the industry is unique 'in that it preserves and encourages the ancient craft of handweaving' (Harris Tweed Association, 1975a). Promotional literature intended for the American market similarly refers to the link between handwoven properties, quality and authenticity, claiming that the industry is still cottage-based (Harris Tweed Association, 1975b). The standard book on the industry shows photographs of traditional processes, spinning-wheels, hand-carding and waulking (shrinking), many dating back to the early years of this century. It also includes details of early dyeing methods using Hebridean flora, mentions Gaelic terms for weaving processes, and records some traditional waulking songs (Thompson, 1969). In all these representations of the industry the accent is on a textile which is handwoven using traditional skills, the product of an individual worker who is not bound by the forces of large-scale factory production.

From early historical accounts of the Hebrides, it seems that weaving was not originally much more than production for domestic use. In the

Lewis Rent Rolls of 1718 rents paid in kind appear as bolls of meal, stirks, chickens or butter and, very occasionally, wool. Nor do any of the later extant Rent Rolls mention rents paid in tweed, and it is unlikely that sub-tenants would have reached an outside market except through the medium of a tacksman or the landlord's factor. This contrasts with the situation in St Kilda where tweed was the main article exported as rent to the factor in the nineteenth century. The only mention of this for Lewis and Harris occurs in the fifteenth century (Steel, 1975, pp. 188–9; Scott Report, 1914, p. 2). Knox's report on the Highlands and Hebrides in 1786 stated categorically that the people had no manufactures and emphasised that fish was their potential wealth. All the crafts he mentions are associated with fishing, the sole exception being a manufacturing house started by the proprietor at Rodil in Harris for spinning woollen thread and twine for herring-nets (Knox, 1787, pp. 26–7, 38, 158). Most of the suggestions made during the nineteenth century for manufacturing on the islands emphasise the possibilities of hemp and flax, and even spinning lint from moss, rather than wool.

The idea of spinning threads other than wool is not surprising. Fleece in any quantity was not available until after the Clearances had produced large sheep-farms. The indigenous crofting population did not depend upon sheep as a major element in their mixed agricultural economy until the early twentieth century. Until then the crofter-fishermen with their cattle, hens and crops of barley and oats, bitterly resented the 'big sheep' which 'devoured' their traditional grazing land.

Of course some sheep were kept, and the fleece was spun and woven for home consumption. Mitchell, writing in 1883, described the people of Lewis as wearing woollen clothes of their own manufacture. The women wore striped or coloured cloth, the men brown or grey, and scarcely any cotton was in use (Mitchell, 1883, 1971, p. 233). Some cloth changed hands on the internal market, and in 1844 the Earl of Dunmore directed some Harris weavers to copy his tartan in tweed. The hardwearing qualities of this tweed recommended it to a wider market. Lady Dunmore and a Mrs Thomas marketed some of the textile in London between 1857 and 1888. The first time a Lewis-made web of cloth was offered for sale outside the Hebrides is reported to have been in 1881 (Scott Report, 1914, pp. 33–4).

Evidence of production for the purely domestic market can still be obtained from the older generation. Many houses contain spinning-wheels, carding implements and occasionally the original ponderous wooden looms. Elderly women describe how wool, clipped from their own sheep, was carded and spun at home. Mosses from the moor were used for dyeing. The thread was stirred in a large pot over the peat fire with all the women in the family taking part in the operations. The work was not always home-based. Washed wool would sometimes be sent to Tarbert, Stornoway or the mainland for carding and spinning. Occasionally, tweeds would be made specifically for mills or for other merchants.

The link with merchants often began because there was a shortage of wool. Weaving was frequently the main occupation of cottars and landless Hebrideans, who lacked the means of agricultural subsistence. By the 1890s merchant finance had penetrated the domestic economy. The factor for Lady Scott of Harris described tweed as the mainstay of cottars and crofters, but added that they were obliged to purchase their supplies of wool from merchants and that this was imported from Leith and Glasgow (Royal Commission (Highlands and Islands), 1892, pp. 1039–40). One crofter from Lochs stated in evidence to the Commission that some people in his village made cloth to sell. He claimed that this was the case in six or seven houses out of a total of twenty built on about a dozen holdings. But the wool was obtained from outside because they had no grazings for sheep. The completed cloth was sold to Duncan MacIver, a Stornoway merchant.

Merchants always paid in kind, so the weavers, like many fishermen, were in perpetual debt. It seemed to the crofter giving evidence that tweed production was not a growth industry, because islanders were forced to purchase wool. In a village near to him weaving was on the decrease because merchants were over-supplied and debts rapidly mounting. This aspect of tweed production added to the inhabitants' demands for more land. Without land they could not graze more sheep, or produce tweed at a profitable rate and become independent of the merchants (ibid, pp. 1008, 1067). Often the loom was also supplied by a merchant, and this added to the crofters' debts. The saying arose that a weaver produced one tweed for himself and two for the loom. The only solution appeared to lie in a commercial selling organisation with considerable working capital.

Just such an organisation was started by Mrs Stewart Mackenzie of Seaforth, and was known as the Crofters' Agency. But the first real breakthrough came with the setting up of the Scottish Home Industries Association as a limited company in 1896. This government organisation abolished the illegal truck or barter system and provided a central source of advances of wool, dyes and essential foodstuffs to the weavers (Scott Report, 1914, p. 45). Merchants resented this interference in their activities, but retaliated by establishing carding-mills to relieve what had become a bottleneck in production. The first mill was built in Tarbert in 1900. Shortly after this, Aeneas Mackenzie set up the first Stornoway mill.

The Scottish Home Industries Association was essentially a government agency. With other State bodies it was attempting to ensure income and employment for Hebrideans. The problem of the redundant population of the Hebrides was no longer regarded as best solved by emigration. Poverty could not be thought of as a failing of the poor. Since the man with no work was now a man with a vote, his problem was conceptualised as 'unemployment' (Gilbert, 1970, p. 51fn). State policy is now orientated towards providing employment in problem areas.

A registered trade-mark ensured that tweed produced in the Western Isles was a unique product protected from outside competition. The holder of the trade-mark is the Harris Tweed Association which was formed in

1909 and began stamping cloth with the mark in 1911. Throughout its chequered legal history the Association has tried to ensure that the Orb Mark (Figure 2) means an adherence to the spirit of a cottage industry. The trade-mark was redefined in 1934 after arguments about the use of mill-spun yarn, and an emphasis placed upon the fact that the cloth was woven at or near the weaver's home. A lengthy court action in 1964 up-held this definition against mainland challenges to the island monopoly of Harris Tweed manufacture.

Advertisements for Harris Tweed imply that it is a traditional textile with the weaver as an independent producer. But early in the history of the industry, carding was a factory process. Spinning then became the major bottleneck, and it was the practice to send wool away to the main-land for one or both operations. By 1906 there were two carding-mills in Stornoway, and the locus of the industry shifted to Lewis. As these mills began to take over spinning, the weavers gradually lost control over the production process. Moreover, there were problems of quality control which related to the type of loom in use and the limited ability of weavers, who had previously produced mainly for domestic purposes. Once a selling organisation had been established it was necessary to ensure a consistent quality of cloth. It was also necessary to produce standard patterns and to provide new patterns for the market.

The type of cloth now produced by the industry bears littls resemblance to that described by Mitchell. There are three standard weights and many colours and patterns of modern design. One mill in particular relies heavily upon the market in female fashions and upholstery materials. The patterns for each year's production are created by professional designers. The warp is made up to specific patterns in the mill (Plate 8) and sent in a mill van

Figure 2. The Orb Mark, trade-mark of the Harris Tweed Association.

Plate 8. Warping in a Stornoway mill.

together with the weft to outworkers. Far from being an independent worker, the weaver is in effect the employee of the mill, despite being classified as self-employed for National Insurance purposes. Although weaving is given prominence in advertising and promotional literature, it represents only a very small proportion of the production process. The wool is purchased by the mills from the Scottish Wool Marketing Board. It is dyed, carded, spun and warped on mill premises (Plate 9). The mills only lose partial control over the production process when the unwoven tweeds travel back and forth across the island to weaving outworkers. Not only are the mills unable to monitor quality, but they also cannot control the time spent weaving. This can cause problems filling orders on time. When the tweeds are ready they are taken back to the mills in mill vans for the finishing processes of darning, fulling and pressing. Finally they are stamped by the Harris Tweed Association with the Orb Mark.

While the mills were still owned by local families the notion of a cottage industry, in which a merchant financier had an interest in marketing the product, was still viable. But in recent years the small family businesses of Stornoway have been progressively taken over or merged until the spinning interests of the island are largely in mainland hands. Only two mills remain in Stornoway out of the many which operated in the 1960s. One is the historical successor to a carding-mill established in 1906. A local family retains managerial functions and controls a proportion of the shares. But the enterprise has been taken over by a mainland group of companies which has a policy of investing in small family firms. The second mill, after a varied history of ownership and control, which at one point aligned it to

Plate 9. Spinning in a Stornoway mill.

multinational interests, now has the Highlands and Islands Development Board as a major shareholder. Only one family firm remains, in the village of Shawbost. Unlike the larger Stornoway mills this company has never sought large markets and bulk orders. It has remained at the optimum size to survive economic recessions. Where small firms went into liquidation through lack of assets in periods of low demand for the cloth, this mill managed to maintain sufficient working capital.

Tweed production has varied over time. From about one million yards a year in 1935 it rose to a maximum of over seven million in 1966. Since then the market has been described as 'in recession'. The combined interests of the mills recently tried to make the industry more competitive in the world textile sphere. They attempted to institute power weaving in order to capture bulk markets. But this would have run counter to another of the implications of the Orb Mark, the assertion that Harris Tweed is handwoven.

The small loom, or *bearst-bheag*, was in use up to the end of the last century. The shuttle was thrown by hand and the yarn wound on sheep's trotter bonds which were used as bobbins. The big loom, *bearst-mhor*, was introduced in 1900. It was worked by hand on the same principle, except that there was a box to receive the shuttle. Through the Congested Districts Board, the State encouraged the use of this 'flying shuttle' loom, and offered interest-free loans for improvement and purchase (Thompson, 1969, p. 68). It was all part of a programme to make the tweed more marketable. Only small webs of tweed with limited use could be produced on ths *bearst-bheag*. The Board employed an instructor, Alexander Lamont, who spent alternate months in Harris and Lewis modernising old looms

and erecting new ones. He had a demonstration loom in his own house and
designed new patterns which he taught to the weavers (Congested Districts
Board, 6th Report 1904, Appendix C, p. 33).

The loom universally used now is the Hattersley Domestic Loom. The
first example of this appeared on the islands in 1912 but it was not until
the 1920s that it began to be generally used. Lord Leverhulme was influential in encouraging its adoption, for it could weave more intricate patterns. Strictly speaking the Hattersley is not a hand-loom. The weaver
simply provides the machine power by working a foot-treadle (Plate 10).
His skill is required to tie-in broken threads and set up and tie-off tweeds
which arrive already warped from the mill. He is the source of power and
the machine minder. He owns the loom, the bobbin-winder and the shed in
which weaving takes place. But access to the market is obtained only
through membership of a special weavers' branch of the Transport and
General Workers' Union, which enables him to have a place on the mills'
distribution list. The weaver is not an independent producer. Nor is he,
properly speaking, a craft worker.

The cloth woven on a Hattersley is not, strictly speaking, handwoven.
The weaver does not touch the cloth except to set up the warp, fill the
bobbins and tie-in broken threads. Far from getting any creative pleasure
from producing the cloth, many dislike the work, seeing it only as an
instrumental means of acquiring a cash income. Isolated in their small huts,
half-deafened by the incessant clatter of the loom, and with their eyes
trained on repetitive patterns like herringbone, many find the job monot-
onous. One weaver stated, 'I put cotton wool in my ears and count the
coin'. Another is reported to have put his loom symbolically outside the
hut and sworn that if tweeds were paid at £100 a time he would never
return to the work. A common description of the task is 'like cycling up-
hill all day long'.

One of the responsibilities of the Harris Tweed Association is to ensure
that no power motors are attached to looms. Some weavers have been
prosecuted for contravention of the legislation. But this condition, laid
down by the Orb Mark, has apparently led to marketing problems. The
Hattersley loom produces cloth which is 'single-width' or twenty-nine
inches wide. In the bulk markets for female clothes and furnishing fabrics
the narrow cloth causes problems for machine cutting. Even hand-cutting
of single-width means a great deal of wastage. In a textile market under
pressure from synthetic fibres this has been blamed for the recession in
demand for Harris Tweed since 1966.

The spinners therefore negotiated for a change in the terms of the Orb
Mark. A double-width hand loom proved too heavy to operate. But the
use of power looms could not be accommodated under the Orb Mark.
After five years of negotiation the spinners, the Weavers' union (the special
Weavers' branch of the TGWU), the Highlands and Islands Development
Board and the Harris Tweed Association put certain proposals before the
weavers. The idea was that double-width power looms would be situated

Plate 10. A weaver at work using a Hattersley loom.

in small factories, called 'workshops', at three points on the island. It is difficult to see how the cloth thus produced would differ from the products of mainland factories. Harris Tweed would have ceased to be a unique, luxury commodity, and in competition with mainland producers would have had the disadvantage of freight charges across the Minch.

When the proposals were put to the weavers in 1976 they were unequivocally vetoed. Without weaver consent the Board of Trade would not alter the conditions of the trade-mark. Plans for power-woven Harris Tweed are in abeyance for a while. The weavers' reasons for refusing to countenance the proposals seemed to rest on a well-justified fear of redundancy. With power looms, output would be raised and unless a large bulk market could be assured many weavers would have been unemployed. The prospect of redundancy payments did not seem sufficient compensation. A further consideration for the weavers was that one of the major advantages of outworking is that it is piece-work. The weaver is effectively in control of his time. The self-employed status means that many have problems with sickness benefit and with maintaining an adequate income when the mills are not busy. But they *can* control the hours during which they work, which would not have been the case in the proposed 'workshops'. For rural weavers with crofts this was an important consideration.

In both fishing and Harris Tweed, therefore, there is no evidence of a static tradition. Both industries have a dynamic history determined partly by State intervention and partly by the influence of external capitalist agencies. They lack security and are under threat from competition in world markets. While they may have specifically Hebridean characteristics they are not traditional sectors of a predominantly modern economy. Nor is the economy of the Western Isles an autonomous entity.

4 The crofting way of life today

Regional policy in the United Kingdom is characterised by a concern to influence the distribution of industry and population. It began with the provision of government credit for industry in 1921 and the organisation of retraining and relocation for the unemployed. But it was only after the Special Areas Act of 1934 that a deliberate geographical definition of problem regions became part of government policy. The main criterion for designation as a Development Area is the existence of an unacceptable level of unemployment. The Highlands of Scotland have long been recognised as an area in which many of the inhabitants were 'redundant', underemployed or unemployed. It was therefore inevitable that it should be given the status of Development Area. In 1965 the Highlands and Islands Development Board was established primarily to increase industrial production in the area, to alleviate unemployment and stem the high rate of outmigration.

Persistent outmigration from the Hebrides has caused both population decline and age-structure imbalance (Tables 1 and 2). The population of the Western Isles as a whole declined by 8 per cent in the period 1961–71,

Table 1. *Population change of the Western Isles and Scotland, 1951–71*

| | Population | | | |
	1951	1961	1971	% change 1951–71
Western Isles	35,591	32,609	29,891	−16
Scotland	5,096,150	5,179,344	5,228,963	+2.6

Source: Census of Population

Table 2. *Age-structure of the Western Isles and Scotland, 1971*

Age-group	% Western Isles	% Scotland
0–14	25.1	26.0
15–44	30.5	38.5
45–59/64	21.3	20.2
60/65+	23.1	15.3

Source: 1971 Census of Population

contrasting with a slight increase in the population of Scotland over the same time. Only Stornoway has experienced an increase in population. Rural areas have become more sparsely populated and smaller islands, which used to be inhabited, are now deserted (Moisley, 1966).

This overall steady decrease in the proportion of people in the fifteen to forty age-group is exacerbated by temporary migrations. Young people move to the mainland for work, either on a seasonal basis or for periods of up to twenty years. Some members of most families are therefore structurally present but physically absent. They may send money home and return for the holidays, or for longer interludes between spells of employment. Occasionally mainland employment can be arranged in such a way that it is possible to return home to take part in essential agricultural tasks. Examples can be found of professional men living in Edinburgh or Glasgow, who return home to the islands during the summer holidays to cut peats for ageing parents. Other family men manage to obtain seasonal work on the mainland and maintain their home base on a croft. But, as seasonal work is usually reliant upon the tourist industry, many active members of rural families are away during the busiest agricultural months of the year. Those who choose to remain on the islands throughout the year are faced with the unemployment situation. The rate of unemployment is difficult to calculate because of the self-employed status of weavers and the pluralism of crofting. For Lewis and Harris it averaged 22.15 per cent in the years 1964–75. But this official figure gives no indication of underemployment. Further important factors are that long-term unemployment is common in the Hebrides, and that the greater proportion of long-term unemployed consists of unskilled men aged over forty-five.

Changes in population size and structure began to take effect on crofting agriculture between the two world wars. In the 1930s the decline of fishing and increase in demand for Harris Tweed also affected crofting activities. In Lewis, weaving took over from fishing as the source of cash income. In Brue every house is reputed to have had a loom during this period, but it was necessary to spend an increasing amount of time weaving, at the expense of agricultural work. Men went to the mainland for seasonal employment. Girls, finding the demand for fish-gutting on the wane, began to leave the island on a more permanent basis, often to work as domestic helps or nurses. Increased educational opportunities made a further drain on the village's human resources. To obtain higher education it was necessary to live in Stornoway during term-time, as the only secondary school in the Hebrides was situated there. For university and training colleges, then as now, one had to travel to the mainland. The opportunities for using this education back in the islands are limited. It is frequently stated that school-teachers are the depopulators of the Hebrides.

Until after the Second World War much of the rhythm of intensive cultivation remained. 'Sheilings' were still used; village cattle continued to provide milk, butter, cream and the coarse cottage cheese known as 'crowdie'. Although flour was seldom milled by villagers, corn and hay were still cultivated for winter fodder. But sheep gradually took over from cattle as the favoured stock. Sheep require less husbandry and are therefore easier for elderly people to manage. As dairy products were no longer made in the home a cash income was required to purchase them from shops. Because the ground was less intensively tilled, it was also necessary to buy winter feed. The family crofting unit therefore needed an income which entailed either the migration of active members or extensive State subsidy. The 77 per cent of the Western Isles which is crofting land was meanwhile becoming increasingly under-productive.

In the 1950s the State provided new crofting legislation and a new Crofters' Commission to combat the picture of depopulation and rural decay. The initial remit of the Commission was to increase productivity and make the marginal agriculture of crofting areas competitive with commercial farming elsewhere. One policy was to amalgamate crofts into 'viable units' and replan villages. This was not attempted in the Western Isles, and resistance to it elsewhere led to the emergence of the Crofters' Union Movement which spread to the Hebrides. The Crofters' Commission then became involved with a scheme started by the North of Scotland College of Agriculture. This did not aim to make crofters competitive with farmers in more favoured areas, but to make crofting agriculture more viable in itself through the individualisation of the croft and better methods of husbandry and cultivation. This has meant that the pattern of crofting has altered from village control towards individual regulation. But it is important to note that it was to some extent the failure of cooperative methods to adapt to new exigencies which led to the growth of individualisation. It cannot be claimed that the imposition of State-sponsored modern methods has broken down communal bonds of mutual aid. In any case it appears that mutual aid in the Hebrides, as elsewhere, is a matter of transactional strategy. The sick and elderly are helped in their domestic and agricultural tasks as a matter of Christian courtesy. But mutual aid given in communal activities is calculated in respect of a return. It is this, rather than kin ties or community spirit, which determines choice of partners in a work group. Over the islands as a whole, reciprocal help has declined as a strategy. There are still set cooperative activities such as sheep-shearing and potato-planting. Where former customs survive it is not in those villages with a high proportion of old people to keep the tradition alive. On the contrary, cooperative patterns are retained in places where there is still a balanced population structure. In other words, a viable community remains communal to some extent. But as fencing grants make individual control of stock and crops a practical proposition it has become more usual for croft work, including peat-cutting, to be a household rather than a family or village matter.

State intervention can in some cases provide the impetus for communal activity. Such was the case in Brue during the early days of the new Crofters' Commission. One of the North of Scotland College of Agriculture schemes which was very successful in Lewis was the reseeding of common pasture. This encouraged more intensive grazing and improved stock. Brue common grazings were largely on moorland peat. The College suggested that this could be reseeded without preliminary ploughing. At first the villagers received this idea with incredulity. But College policy is to demonstrate that new ideas work and then to allow crofters to continue on their own initiative. The College Advisor on Lewis at the time began to reseed an area within sight of Brue. 'Everyone thought he was crazy', remarked one of the older men. After three years the experiment proved a success. With the help of Crofters' Commission grants the villagers set to work on thirty-eight acres of common grazings. 'The whole village turned out to put down the sand. We did it by hand, a string of about thirty of us with buckets. We did the same with the seed and fertilizer.' This, and two further schemes were successful so long as the new growth of grass was grazed correctly. But the pressures which led to the partial breakdown of the project reflect again the influence of external commercial necessities.

The correct way to graze the new pasture would be with cattle in the summer, followed by short periods with sheep. This is because sheep are selective feeders. Left to themselves they eat only the short grasses. Coarse grass gradually gains ascendancy and the pasture deteriorates. Older people and those who are in full-time employment find it more convenient to limit their stock to sheep. The grazing of communal apportionments of reseeded pasture thus presents a problem. It has become more common for people to make application to the Crofters' Commission for individual apportionments of common grazing. The areas thus improved by reseeding can be seen all over the island as small, fenced areas of moorland, noticeably greener than the surrounding heather. Strangely enough, the sheep which were the original cause of evictions and distress in the nineteenth century are now ubiquitous.

Although some hay and other crops are harvested throughout the islands, much winter feed is now purchased. The uncertain climate creates harvesting difficulties for people in full-time employment. Methods of harvesting which would make storing the crop less difficult, such as making silage, have not been accepted. One crofter objected to the smell of silage. He did not want to smell 'like a farmer'. Even the arable infield is now often only used as grazing for stock. In many cases older people who no longer cultivate their lots lease their ground, officially or unofficially, to neighbours or kin. Of the twenty-eight crofts in Brue, twenty-one were still worked in 1976. The degree of intensiveness varied from one man who kept twenty-three head of cattle, to families tending a patch of potatoes for their own use. Six of the crofts, and one feu on a croft, were sublet. Five of these were leased to people within the village and two to people outside the village who had kinship links. At least three of the crofts were worked with the help of children who no longer resided permanently in the village.

This picture of crofting activity in Lewis is not uniform throughout the Western Isles. In Uist, where the crofts are larger and land more fertile, it is possible for crofting to be a more full-time occupation. The increase in the number of sheep and decrease in the number of cows kept is typical of Lewis but not of the other islands (Table 3). The islanders in the south of the Hebrides tend to keep one or more cows on the croft and are thus more or less self-sufficient in dairy production, except for butter which few women trouble to make. In Lewis even milk is imported from the mainland, although there are small local dairy farms. Where a cow is kept, milk, cream and 'crowdie' are the main products. When a cow is in milk following the birth of a calf, there is often a surplus over household requirements. Milk is then shared with, or sold to, other residents in the village. Islanders elsewhere in the Hebrides are conscious of the differences in animal husbandry in Lewis. In Scalpay a woman who was proud of her cow's capacity to produce milk mocked Lewis husbandry. 'They don't even have a bull in Lewis.' The 'Harris bull', of which there are several, is moved from village to village to serve cows, and is the object of attention wherever he goes. In Lewis it is usual for those crofters who keep a cow to use the subsidised artificial insemination service provided by the Department of Agriculture and Fisheries (Plate 11).

It seems that, in general, crofts are becoming less important for their agricultural value and more important as sites for homes. This is aided to some extent by generous grants and loans from State sources. A common sight in the Hebrides is the residential caravan sited close to a crofting home. This is often the home of a young couple, children of the official crofter, who are saving-up to build their own house on the croft (Plate 12). This adds to the family labour available for croft work. A further familiar sight is the empty, and occasionally abandoned, house on crofting land (Plate 13). In some cases, croft houses are used only when a family returns from the mainland in the summer months. Sometimes the house is rented to newcomers to the village or island. The crofting land will be sublet as grazing to another member of the community. In still other cases the house-and-garden site is placed on a separate tenancy and the croft worked as a detached unit by another individual. This is effectively the same as the situation in which an elderly person lives in the house and sublets the croft land.

Table 3. *Livestock per crofting unit in the Western Isles, 1975*

Area	Cows per unit	Sheep per unit
Lewis	0.28	22.61
Harris	1.01	44.12
North Uist	3.02	20.54
South Uist, Benbecula & Eriskay	2.52	16.46
Barra & Vatersay	0.85	9.49
Western Isles average	0.93	22.64

Source: Western Isles Regional Report

Plate 11. The single cow kept on this Harris croft is tethered close to the settlement.

Plate 12. Croft housing in Lewis.

Plate 13. Derelict house on crofting land.

The Crofters (Scotland) Act of 1976 has given the crofter the right to purchase his croft from the landlord, although much common grazing will remain vested in the landlord with crofters having tenurial rights as before. It has been suggested that this development of crofting land into a commodity will lead to the decline of its agricultural use and make it possible for unscrupulous property developers to make profits at the expense of the indigenous population. One of the motivations behind the Act was an appeal to ancient rights of ownership. Another was that the security of ownership would increase agricultural activity and the overall productivity of crofting areas. But there has been no rush of applications from crofters to purchase their holdings, and this may be related to the reluctance of Lewis crofters to accept the free gift offered by Leverhulme.

There seem to be two main motivations for crofters when they consider the 1976 Act. First there is a distrust of legislation, a feeling that there 'must be a catch in it'. Crofting legislation has always been complex and difficult to understand, even for legal experts. The Crofters' Commission and other interested bodies did try to disseminate information about the Act in crofting areas through public meetings, leaflets and newspaper articles. But crofters appear unwilling to risk losing the grants and loans, to which they are entitled under the old system, in favour of the dubious pleasure and added responsibility of being owner-occupiers. A second reason is that some crofters feel they should not be asked to purchase a legal right to which they already claim a moral right. 'It's wrong to build your house and then have no title to it, but there's another moral argument.

My relations hacked that croft out of the soil and took the stones for the house. Now I'm being asked to buy it as if the landlord had done all this.'

The changing pattern of crofting agriculture over the past two centuries has been towards progressive individualisation. This has not been the result of modernity making incursions into a static tradition. On the contrary, it is part of a dynamic combination of strategies. The State has the major economic strategy of maximisation of the wealth of the nation as a whole. In the United Kingdom this is motivated by the economics of growth. This has led to the development of special policies for areas which become relatively impoverished with respect to more prosperous areas. The work of the Highlands and Islands Development Board has been primarily oriented towards developing the Highland Region through the tenets of growth economics. It has defined the area as underdeveloped or marginal because of a low level of industrialisation and a high level of unemployment. The remedy is inevitably seen to be a redistribution of industry. But, because of the definition of the Highlands as a culturally homogenous region, such industrial development has to be compatible with the 'crofting way of life'. This involves the Board in a contradiction which was apparent even in the recommendations of an earlier Scottish Committee:

(1) The conditions of life in which work will be carried out in the Highlands must be made to approximate so far as possible to conditions elsewhere.
(2) Inequalities due to distance from centres of consumption must be minimised by attention to Communications and Freight Charges.
(3) The application of modern methods, and the utilization of scientific discovery must be energetically pursued and demonstrated in the interests of Agriculture, Fishing and Forestry.
(4) Industries appropriate to the area, and in harmony with the Highland temperament must be established, and the great part which Water Power can take in this development must be examined to the full (Scottish Economic Committee, 1938, p. 28).

The importance of this unrecognised contradiction between growth industry and crofting culture can be appreciated if it is remembered that both contradictory elements are used in the legitimation of decisions. Highlands and Islands Development Board policy maintains and intensifies the idea of a special way of life while advocating growth and development of a type characteristic of the industrial south of England. The idea of a static crofting way of life is used to legitimate developmental plans to which it is logically opposed. Yet within government policy the two are treated as if they are mutually reinforcing. Even the new Crofters' Commission soon found itself in the position of maintaining a 'tradition' while attempting modernisation (Gillanders, 1968, pp. 100ff.) and ceased to concentrate exclusively on the agricultural side of crofting. By 1966 the Commission was advocating a possible symbiosis of crofting and industry.

In 1959 a government review likewise rejected the idea of a crofting economy based on agricultural pursuits. It claimed that 'the prosperity of the Highlands is an essential element in the well-being of the nation' and that industrial development in the area is necessary to the attainment of a balanced economy (*Review of Highland Policy*, 1959, pp. 2, 8). By 1974 the Crofters' Commission was criticising the primarily agricultural concerns of the European Economic Community's directive on farming in less-favoured areas, and maintaining that the 'solution of crofting agricultural problems should be sought through the provision of non-agricultural employment in the crofting areas rather than the redistribution of agricultural land' (Crofters' Commission, 1974, pp. 2–3).

The importance of the establishment of the Highlands and Islands Development Board was that it represented a rationalisation and streaming of the multiplicity of agencies previously working in the area. It was perhaps unfortunate that none of the original members of the Board spoke Gaelic or was well acquainted with the problems of the Western Isles. Until 1977 it had no permanent office in Stornoway and its activities and decisions seemed remote to Hebridean residents. The board believed that the task of producing a balanced economy and full employment could be best achieved through the development of growth centres. It was soon engaged in establishing the mainland area of Invergordon as an industrial complex. Possibly the most apt description of the Board was given by its second Chairman, Sir Andrew Gilchrist, when he called it 'a merchant bank with a social purpose' (*North* 7, 1971, p. 3). Much of the literature produced by the Board extols the potential of the Highlands and Islands for development by external industrial interests. Its policy statements refer to the stimulation of growth, the stabilisation of population and the provision of employment.

Local people in the Hebrides were well aware of the priority given by the Board to the attraction of 'foreign' interests. On more than one occasion the opinion has been expressed that if an Englishman went to the Board's offices in Inverness asking for a large grant for an ambitious project in the Western Isles it would be granted, whereas a local man asking for a few hundred pounds to invest in an already existing business would be turned down. Moreover, some individuals can quote a list of Board-funded projects which have subsequently failed. Small factories intended to attract incoming industrialists were built near Stornoway, which was designated the growth area for the Western Isles. But these stood empty for some time before being utilised, largely by local concerns. A common island attitude towards the 'Highland Board' is scorn and mistrust.

The symbiotic relationship between crofting agriculture, fishing and weaving is frequently assumed to be the ideal combination for maintaining the 'crofting way of life'. But as has already been seen, fishing is now a full-time occupation and provides employment for a relatively small percentage of the population. Harris Tweed production occupies only about 17 per cent of the employed population. This includes mill workers in Stornoway who suffer frequent lay-offs and short-week working and who have experienced major redundancies since the production peak of 1966. Many crofters in rural areas of Lewis weave tweeds on their crofts, but fluctuations in demand during the year make their income unreliable. By weaving three tweeds a week it is possible to maintain a reasonable standard of living. But weaving at this rate is virtually a full-time job which leaves little free time for croft work. Full-time weavers are concentrated in Stornoway. The major proportion of Harris Tweed is woven in small huts situated close together near Stornoway council houses.

The mills use distribution lists to spread weaving work throughout the island. In 1976 only three weavers produced Orb-Marked tweed in Harris, and there are problems in transporting outwork so far afield. In times of low demand many weavers may only receive one tweed a fortnight. In remoter rural areas the distribution of tweeds often appears erratic and arbitrary. Weavers say that they are 'grateful for a tweed' when it arrives. Many of those in the more distant villages express the opinion that weavers in Stornoway and surrounding areas are given preference by the mills.

The symbiosis of crofting, fishing and weaving is therefore largely mythical. Some crofters do manage to eke out a living from their agricultural land, together with making the occasional web of cloth, and fishing. But it should be remembered that crofting agriculture is State-subsidised. Besides grants and loans for building houses and fencing and reseeding, there are subsidies available for sheep and cattle husbandry. It cannot be claimed that this way of life is economically viable from the point of view of the State. The productive power of Hebridean labour adds little to the gross national product and does not balance the large amount of direct and indirect State subsidy received by islanders. Other forms of employment in the area are limited in scope. Many island men are employed in the construction industry. But a large proportion of these are in local authority employ, and the three largest construction firms are frequently contracted to build local authority housing.

Over 50 per cent of those in employment in the Western Isles are engaged in the tertiary or service sector. With the exception of the small proportion in tourism, these workers do not generate any income for the islands as a whole. Tourism has increased in importance but the short summer season is a disadvantage. Further problems are presented by the difficulty and expense of travel across the Minch. Another factor is the climate and relative lack of recreation and leisure facilities. Even Stornoway now has no cinema. Hotels, bars and restaurants are unevenly and thinly spread through the islands and Sabbath closing is the norm. Many islanders provide bed and breakfast accommodation in their own homes, which produces extra income in the tourist season. But the potential for tourism in the Outer Hebrides has yet to be fully realised.

The remainder of those employed in the service sector are engaged in shop work, office work and transport, or as teachers, doctors and other professionals. A major source of income is once again the State.

All these types of employment can be, and are, combined with crofting. Many people commute quite long distances to the major centres of work, such as Stornoway, and perform agricultural tasks in the evenings and on

Saturdays, often with the help of family and neighbours. This can mean that the rhythm of the countryside penetrates the busy and often cosmopolitan atmosphere of Stornoway.

There is a certain opposition, even antagonism, between the rural and urban areas of Lewis. The cattle grids which cross the outgoing roads from the town often appear to have a symbolic significance. Stornoway is different in terms of the entertainment and facilities it provides, as well as being the administrative and employment centre. This is summed-up in the language-use distinction. Many Stornowegians do not speak Gaelic, nor want to speak it. Until recently many of those who were fluent in the language would not admit it for fear of being labelled country-dwellers. Rural areas, on the other hand, become increasingly dominated by the use of Gaelic as one moves further away from the town. Even in English usage country-dwellers complain about the clipped, nasal Stornowegian accent. Their comments and often accurate imitations show a distrust of town-dwellers.

But many of those who work in the town do not live there. Networks of relationship and gossip spread throughout the islands and permeate the workplace, as do the exigencies of crofting activity. Office work appears more casual than that typical in the growth areas of the United Kingdom. But it is not necessarily less efficient. There is little of the ideology of 'being busy' and office workers will seldom state that they 'have no time' to deal with a query or request. Individual needs are taken into account. This means that business is dealt with 'on the spot' with the minimum of delay and bureaucracy. It can also mean that on any sunny spring morning one may see rural-based office workers driving *out* of town at 9.30 a.m. They are on their way to do the ploughing or cut peat, having dealt briefly with the morning's post.

Although the agricultural aspects of the crofting way of life are not a major component in occupational pluralism they have strong ideological associations. To islanders, crofting means a particular emotional attachment to the Hebrides. The idea of the crofting way of life evokes the history of land struggles. But, more than this, crofting provides an occupational base-line, a continuity within a shifting employment pattern. The occupational pluralism of the Western Isles is not one-dimensional. There is a longitudinal aspect. Adherence to any one industrial category is not characteristic of individual life experience. The arrival of oil-related industry on the island in 1973 provided an example of this.

The enterprise in question, Lewis Offshore Ltd, was the branch development of a Norwegian group of companies. During the 'North Sea Oil Boom' of the early 1970s, it leased ninety-three acres of land south of Stornoway and proposed to initiate a development which would employ 1,000 workers by 1981. As the total of registered unemployed workers in Lewis at the time was 1,100, Lewis Offshore appeared to be the answer to the island's economic problems. The firm also gave an undertaking to employ local labour as far as possible and established training programmes in welding and related trades. The workforce did rise to 500 at one point and attracted many locally-born men back from the mainland. Some largely job-specific training was provided. But by 1978 the workforce was redundant. Lewis Offshore had been affected by the general dearth of orders in oil-related production. Many mainland platform construction yards were also idle and Lewis Offshore appeared to have been yet another case of 'boom and slump' for the Hebrides.

Lewis Offshore workers showed many examples of the shifting work history of individual islanders. One bachelor in his thirties gave the following life history:

I left school wanting a job to come back to Lewis, but there were no possibilities here for a technical training. I went to Glasgow at nineteen, working as a supervisor in an office. I'd never been to Glasgow before, and I wasn't very impressed with the environment. It was totally foreign to me. Black dusty buildings. The people were O.K. but I couldn't stick being in an office. I came back to an office here with Mc———. I didn't like that for the same reasons. But I didn't have any proper qualifications so I had to take clerical work and stick to that for two years. Then I was a mobile-shop driver for three years. I was still cooped-up inside, but the people were different every day. Then I was a builder's labourer for two years. I enjoyed that and was quite happy, but I decided to leave as I didn't want to do it for the rest of my life. Then I applied to Lewis Offshore.

This islander was employed on the shop floor for nearly the whole of the Company's short life. Another older, married man, who joined Lewis Offshore some time later, stated:

My first job on leaving school was on a Stornoway boat. I was just a nipper. That was till 1939. I joined the forces in 1943 in May, until 1944. Then I had a job with the Department of Agriculture in Lewis, ploughing all over the island. It's a healthy life. I did that for three years. The next step was the Harris Tweed industry. Driving, delivering tweeds, for twenty-two years. By then I was living in Stornoway. I worked with ——— and then with ———. It was a busy job. Then they were taken over by a firm from England, so there were redundancies. Around 1970. But I was tired of driving anyway. It was long enough at the same thing. From there I went to ———, a contracting business, a Glasgow firm, driving too. But it was difficult to get back from there [the mainland], I was losing time. I went to an American firm at Invergordon for about nine months, then to Nigg Bay [oil-platform construction yards]. I was there for a year-and-a-half. It was very good, but I came back when the work started here. I was working with that firm from England, Bovis [building construction]. Now I'm at Lewis Offshore.

These life histories might seem to be indicative of certain comments in the Highland Home Industries Report of 1914 that those with the 'Celtic temperament' cannot settle to any one occupation for long (Scott Report, 1914, p. 81). But it is more likely that lack of skilled-job opportunities leads to these shifting patterns. Both the men quoted above were able and intelligent individuals capable of the sort of skilled employment for which neither training nor opportunity had been available unless they had chosen to sever the connection with their island home.

One attitude of semi-skilled or unskilled workers in the Hebrides is revealed in the comment: 'It was long enough at the same thing'. Where skills are few and jobs tend to be impermanent there can also be a sense of impermanence about the attitude to work. This is exacerbated by the islands' employment situation. There are periodic booms in employment opportunities. Occasionally these are caused by short-lived industrial enterprises. More typically they are provided by the construction of major public works such as hydro-electricity plants, the NATO base at Stornoway or the missile-testing range at Benbecula. Thus, besides engaging in temporary migration to obtain employment and skills on the mainland, many islanders are used to periods of unemployment alternating with periods of varied types of employment.

The island workforce seems to have an attitude of flexibility. Employers often comment on the Hebridean's willingness to attempt any kind of task. Yet this is coupled with a somewhat cynical approach to work which may give an impression of idleness to the outsider. Work is often regarded as short-term, varied, impermanent and insecure. For men in most Western societies employment status provides the main thread of continuity in adult life. But being a man in the Western Isles does not necessarily equate with being a 'breadwinner' or wage-earner. The reference group for masculine identity and status is principally external to the work situation. Yet it is not only officially-designated crofters who are able to maintain a masculine identity. Rather it is partaking, even symbolically, in the crofting way of life which bestows a form of island integrity. This can be as true of Stornoway dwellers as it is of those in remote rural districts for whom crofting is a full-time activity. There are few native islanders who have no attachment to a crofting area. Crofting is the base-line of all other economic activities. As an idea it provides the secure focus for an insecure existence.

5 The heirs of the Land League

Lewis Grassic Gibbon once referred to the history of Scotland as being divided into the phases of 'Colonization, Civilization and Barbarization'. He added: 'That the last word is a synonym for Anglicization is no adverse reflection upon the quality of the great English culture' (Grassic Gibbon, 1934, p. 19). The stage of 'Barbarization' may be thought of as commencing with the Act of Union in 1707. This ratified the position of the Scottish economy as an integral part of developing English capitalism. It also shifted the effective power base from Edinburgh southwards to London. The Scottish aristocracy and middle classes became involved in a new set of social and economic relations. As explained in Chapter 2, one result was the Clearances which led to the creation of the Highland Land League.

The original League lost its cohesion because the leaders could not agree on the Irish Home Rule question, which was closely related to Highland concerns. It was an issue which divided those who thought Highland problems could be solved by Scottish independence, from those who were more interested in an immediate practical solution to the land issue. This division is still a feature of national politics as experienced in Scotland and in the Western Isles. In the 1890s the polarisation of this debate led to such disarray in the Land League that landlords and factors were returned in local elections in the Hebrides where, a short while before, crofter candidates had been successful. The League's prevarication over the extent of its own radicalism led to the collapse of its political activity into Liberalism and London-based control. But land agitation continued throughout the Highlands.

More radical alternative parties, like the Scottish Land Restoration League, put forward parliamentary candidates, but their support was largely urban. Meanwhile, as land reform was espoused as a cause by the Liberals, it became necessary for the labour movement to form an alternative party. Industrial and rural proletarian interests combined to form the Scottish Labour Party which later became affiliated to the British Labour Party. The Highland Land League was revived on two further occasions. It was finally reconstituted in 1921 as the Scots National League which eventually became part of the Scottish National Party.

It was not until the 1930s that the Scottish National Party emerged in its present form. Since that time nationalism has progressed in two parallel directions. There have been successive waves of electoral success for the

60

party itself, and there is a steady rise in national consciousness. The initial electoral success of the party in the 1930s was the political accompaniment of severe economic depression in Scotland. Scottish industrial development after the Act of Union depended upon heavy industry. But after the First World War the United Kingdom output of heavy industry and its share of the world market declined. The proportional importance of Scotland in the British economy decreased. England partly recovered by developing newer industries, but Scotland was too far from the larger urban markets and lacked the capital to invest in light industry. New forms of Scottish employment tended to be in the unproductive service sector. The Labour vote in Scotland collapsed and for the first time it was appreciated that a vote for a nationalist organisation could be effective.

The political success of the Scottish National Party has taken place against the background of relative economic deprivation, rising unemployment, outmigration and lower wages than in England. The policies of regional development produced by the 1964 Labour government did not appreciably improve the situation. Increasing electoral success by nationalist parties led to other political parties investigating the possibility of increasing the degree of devolution within the United Kingdom. A White Paper called *Our Changing Democracy* was published in November 1975 recommending a degree of legislative devolution as the only practical way to transfer power from the centre to the regions. It suggested the creation of a single-chamber Scottish Assembly empowered to pass laws on a variety of devolved subjects such as local government, law, health and education, and able to raise extra revenue from local taxation. The major source of finance would be a block grant from British taxation, which the Scottish Assembly could reallocate as it wished. But the Secretary of State for Scotland, responsible to central government, would remain with powers of veto (*Our Changing Democracy*, 1975).

At present Britain is a 'composite of jurisdictions joined in one state'. As each of these jurisdictions has a sense of communal identity, which is used to justify the separation of their institutions, the most suitable description of Britain is probably that of multinational state (Rose, 1970, pp. 1–2). Various forms of devolution already exist above local government level. Between 1920 and 1972, when direct rule was imposed, Northern Ireland possessed its own executive, local government structure and courts in a semi-federal relationship. The Channel Islands and the Isle of Man have certain separate institutions. Wales, while having no separate legal system or political institutions, constitutes a distinct area. There is a Welsh Office, Secretary of State and Grand Committee. Scotland has a position midway between Wales and Northern Ireland. While it has possessed no autonomous government or parliament since 1707, it still has a 'strong constitutional identity', retains its own legal system, Established Church, educational system and local authorities. A Scottish Office was established in 1885, a Secretary of State has a permanent place in the Cabinet, and since 1894 a Scottish Grand Committee has existed to pass

Scottish Bills. There are usually between five and ten in each parliamentary session (Kellas, 1973, pp. 1—2). The Secretary of State personifies Scottish government, but he also has a proconsular role, representing Scotland in London and London in Scotland. He is always chosen by the majority party in Westminster rather than Scotland (ibid, p. 75).

Our Changing Democracy is the pivot of political thought on national issues in the Western Isles in the 1970s. Devolution has been debated by all political parties, and Bills have been presented to the House of Commons. But it was *Our Changing Democracy* which provided the basic material for argument even though the Secretary of State for Scotland at the time commented that it was 'more discussed than read' (*Guardian*, 6 January 1976). The Western Isles were no exception. But the islanders have an ambivalent nationalism. They seem to feel the need for Celtic or Hebridean independence as much as that for Scottish separatism.

The political heirs of the Land League are the Labour Party in Scotland and the Scottish National Party. This apparent contradiction is highlighted in the Western Isles where the labour movement, historically and conceptually, has been involved in nationalist ideology and the middle class is often symbolised not as 'capitalists' but as 'Englishmen'. The Western Isles constituency was the first electoral success for the Scottish National Party in a general election. Prior to this the islands had returned a Labour MP to parliament for thirty-five years. One of the underlying issues in the changeover is admitted by many islanders to be that of personality. It was more an expression of dissatisfaction with a particular Labour MP than with the tenets of socialism.

Personality is a vital component in this small constituency. At this level even national politics work on a face-to-face basis. The character, family and history of the Member of Parliament were well known by acquaintance and gossip to his 29,000 constituents. He was a familiar figure in the islands and had worked his way up in local-government politics before standing for parliament. Many people in Stornoway can remember him from school and recall his work in a local mill. His reputation as an honest local man is possibly the highest political card he holds. There is an acceptance in the islands that they have only a single voice in the corridors of Westminster and they wish it to be a Hebridean voice.

The Scottish National Party now commands a high degree of loyalty in the islands and the Labour Party lacks both regular membership and funds. After its defeat by the nationalists and until 1976 it also lacked a prospective candidate with local connections and continued to lose elections to the nationalists. Many older socialists express the feeling that political activity has declined. In the past, elections were major events in which it seemed that the entire adult population was involved. There were street marches and activities and public meetings which presented ample opportunity for practising the art of oratory. In the words of one Labour supporter, 'We knew what we were fighting for. Now people have forgotten the issues.'

The new Labour candidate was a local man with extensive political experience and a reputation for being a 'good man to have on your side'. Confrontation between the two parties was inevitable. Both Conservative and Liberal parties are at present overshadowed, although there is an extensive history of liberalism in the islands. Scottish Nationalist supporters take an aggressive stance which seems to be a new element in island politics. It is a revival of the protesting spirit of the Land League which feeds on feelings of dispossession. Paradoxically this is not necessarily always linked to a demand for Scottish independence. Many islanders state that they would rather be ruled from London than Edinburgh. Scottish independence might mean that the combined voices of industrial Scotland would drown the single voice of the Western Isles. The problem of being a deprived minority with special difficulties could be lost in overall plans to improve the conditions of the deprived majority of Lowland Scotland.

Yet the islanders channel their feelings of deprivation, through nationalist rhetoric, towards the English. Conceptually the English have become the middle class and the class struggle is subverted by the nationalist struggle. It is not uncommon to hear even the most sophisticated Labour supporter imply that all Englishmen vote Conservative. The Scottish National Party is able to appeal to all sections of the community by providing a de-ideologising ideology. It can appeal to those who previously voted Conservative by emphasising the relative lack of control Scottish capital exercises over enterprises based in Scotland. It can also appear radical because it does not detail its policies. While eschewing talk of class warfare it can claim to be egalitarian (Wolfe, 1973, p. 147) and mentions legislation to administer 'social justice' and a fairer distribution of wealth (ibid, p. 137). It therefore enjoys considerable working-class support. Research tends to show that many Scots vote for the Scottish National Party while maintaining a lifelong identification with other political parties. There is no simpler nor more effective political creed than one which ascribes a wide range of difficulties and grievances to one primary cause.

The nationalist revival in the Western Isles can be viewed as a class conflict in which the entire population of the Western Isles conceives of itself as proletarian in one respect: the feeling of deprivation. Internal divisions of class are not evident despite disparity of wealth between individual families. *Comhairle nan Eilean*, the Western Isles Islands Council, is not officially organised along party lines, although the political sympathies of councillors are often clear during discussions at council meetings. When elections for public office other than that of Member of Parliament take place, candidates are nominated on the basis of their suitability for the task rather than their political persuasion. But *Comhairle nan Eilean* is often concerned with subjects like the level of Rate Support Grant received from central government. These underline the area's relative deprivation and much of the discussion takes a proto-nationalist form. This is the case despite the predominantly left-wing council membership. It may be related to the lack of cohesion of socialists on the council, which is possibly due to the explicit exclusion of party politics from local government.

Alongside the apparent lack of class consciousness at the level of political activity there is a noticeable absence of that class gradation in social relationships which typifies English rural and urban life. There is a certain rural/urban antagonism between country areas and Stornoway. There is much rivalry between areas. The islands to the south resent the relatively greater administrative capacity and economic advantages found on Lewis. In rural communities some individuals are set apart in interaction. In protestant areas this is connected to the lack of a pastoral role for ministers and the separation between secular and sacred spheres. But in the Roman Catholic south the priest also has a noticeably separate social life. Communicant members of the Presbyterian Churches tend to form a distinctively cohesive group. Teachers and others who have received higher education are respected for their qualifications, but this only confers a higher status for certain purposes. They may be active as crofters and their place in the daily life of the village may be a function of this, rather than of a position within an external employment structure. On the other hand the qualifications and the job will be the subject of comment and appraisal. This leads to a further set of role expectations within the village. These are the people who are most likely to be nominated for local committees. They are also likely to be asked to perform bureaucratic tasks for other villagers, such as providing help filling-in official forms.

Stornoway does have clearly defined residential areas which can be designated in terms of wealth. Wealth in itself does not confer either respect or status upon an individual. But it is the subject of constant gossip and comment. In rural areas the amount of inter-house visiting may vary from village to village, but the type and quality of other people's possessions and new acquisitions are evergreen topics of conversation. Older people claim that this is the result of materialistic attitudes and that things used to be otherwise. Certainly many of the items considered necessities in the rest of Britain are relatively new in the islands. Electricity has only arrived in some areas during the past few decades, and thus household electrical appliances are novelties of a kind. Television has only relatively recently provided daily reminders of the ways of life and material conditions of other areas of Britain, as well as in Europe and America.

Household and even clothing purchases are major events for any family because of the difficulties of supply. Many of the larger or more exclusive items have to be bought on the mainland and transported to the islands at considerable expense. Any trip to the mainland is thus a much-discussed opportunity for shopping and commissions are usually undertaken for friends and kin. Mail-order catalogues are much in use and, as the agent is usually a neighbour or relation, the item purchased and its price cannot be kept secret. Groups of friends or relations often combine to make shopping expeditions to Stornoway and goods will be discussed on the journey home. In addition, most areas are served by mobile shops of all descriptions and these shopkeepers are an abundant source of gossip. One described this part of his work as 'a social service'.

It is difficult for anyone to impress his fellow islanders with the extent of his purchases or the size of his house. Local men, who have returned to the island to take up official positions after gaining educational qualifications, are particularly liable for criticism of their life-style. The qualifications may be much admired, even boasted of, and it will be said with pride that it is good to see a local man rather than a foreigner in an important administrative position. But at the same time, individuals who have returned, to take up employment as officials of the new council for instance, will be subjected to much criticism and resentment. They will be watched to see that they do not 'get above themselves'. This observation can be made of local returners to any area, but in the Hebrides it is compounded with the sensitivity wrought of many years of experiencing the sensations of dispossession and deprivation. The individual is judged on his behaviour, not his possessions.

It might be expected that there would be some feelings of class antagonism expressed towards the landlords of those estates on Lewis which still remain in private ownership. Many of these proprietors are absentees except during holiday or sporting seasons. Perhaps it could be claimed that poaching is an expression of hostility, as Emmett noted was the case in North Wales. But landlords are usually conceptualised as English rather than aristocratic. Proletarian and nationalist sentiment remain combined. On the other hand, English residents who settle on the island are usually treated with admirable courtesy. In the abstract they are sometimes combined with settlers from the Scottish mainland and referred to as 'white settlers' or even 'the English'. Yet new residents are often welcomed into local communities. Each case is treated on its merits, and different individuals within the same family are often given separate treatment. It seems that adult males usually integrate better than females, whereas among children girls are more easily assimilated than boys. If people are willing to observe local customs and take part in village activities they can often integrate quite well. Yet any suspicion that the newcomer will try to impose foreign ways on local people will be strongly resented.

Newcomers often react strongly towards religion, particularly in the northern islands. Hunter has claimed that throughout the Highlands the development of evangelical puritanism was a political phenomenon (Hunter, 1974b, p. 95). He asserts that revivals took place in the early nineteenth century because religious symbolism and the integrative power of ritual replaced the confusion and disorder which followed the disintegration of the clan system. Throughout the Highlands, religious experience provided relief from suffering and frustration. The revivals also produced their own grass-roots leadership, known as 'the Men'. These indigenous religious orators disputed with the ministers of the Established Church of Scotland over the interpretation of the Scriptures. More importantly for Hunter's argument they defied the patronage system by which landlords could foist their own choice of minister on tenants. In doing this the Men implicitly challenged the ideological bases of the tenurial system.

The climax to this dispute came in 1843 when the Free Church of Scotland split away from the Established Church. Almost the entire Lewis population joined forces with the Free Church. Although the 1843 Disruption was essentially a Lowland phenomenon, which reflected the relationship between Edinburgh and Westminster, it struck a chord of dissent in the remote Western Isles. Congregations, lay preachers and some ministers abandoned the buildings and tenets of the Established Church. They lacked churches of their own but worshipped in the open until they had raised enough money to erect their own buildings. Proprietors attempted to prevent them obtaining land and there were financial problems for ministers who had left relatively comfortable livings in the Established Church. The salaries of dissenting ministers were paid in cash and kind by their congregations.

Hunter claims that the 1843 Disruption was less an ecclesiastical and theological dispute than a class conflict. He points to the proprietorial opposition to the development of the Free Church and to links between religious leaders and the Land League. Land League meetings often resembled the open-air assemblies of the Free Church. The membership was similar. Hunter states that 'the local leaders of the Land League . . . occupied positions in the townships that were in all respects analogous to those held by "the Men" of a preceding generation' (ibid, p. 108). Land League meetings were often addressed by a catechist and frequently held in the houses of Church elders. The Free Church was able to give a sacred legitimation to demands for land-law reform. The Minister for Lochs stated to a commission of inquiry into crofting conditions that every man had a God-given right to the land which no landlord could usurp (Royal Commission (Highlands and Islands), 1892, p. 1072). A letter in the *Highland News* in 1893 claimed that 'The Highland Land League teaches a political economy which is only Utopian to those to whom the Sermon on the Mount is Utopian' (*Highland News*, 13 May 1893).

This early revivalist spirit quickly became institutionalised in some respects. But the evangelistic fervour remains. The Free Church grew in economic strength, purchasing leases on land and building churches and manses. It also gained a hold on the education system in Lewis, partly because central government was unable to administer the 1872 Education (Scotland) Act efficiently in this remote area. One teacher arriving in Lewis in 1881 was told before his journey that unless he was a Free Church member he need not trouble to apply for a post (Patterson, 1970, p. 159). At the turn of the century there were many sectarian shifts and realignments in the Lewis Churches. Although these were ostensibly caused in the interpretation of the Bible they frequently took the form of disagreements over buildings and landholdings. On one occasion a Stornoway congregation was evicted from its place of worship after a lawsuit brought by a minority secession group (Calder, 1913, pp. 11–14).

The relationship between State and Church, between the secular and sacred spheres, which was at the heart of the Disruption, continued to be discussed on the island. A leading Stornoway minister wrote in 1913 that:

It was because the State on the ground of the alliance that existed between it and the Church and on the ground that it supported the Church out of the national resources, insisted on ruling the Church that the Church separated from the State. It was because the Church believed that the State insisted on ruling her, in some things at least, contrary to the mind of Christ, that she severed her connection with the State at the Disruption and gave up all State emoluments in order to be free to obey Christ as she interpreted His mind in the scriptures (ibid, p. 17).

Yet in recent years two distinct attitudes towards the role of religion in life have developed on the island. One seeks to divide the sacred from the secular and becomes increasingly inward-looking. The other is heir to the symbolic legitimation of the political creed of Land Leaguism and requires the active participation of the Church in the political sphere.

The focus of both attitudes is often conceptualised by outsiders and unbelievers as Sabbath observance. The rigidity of this observance in the protestant north of the Western Isles is frequently given as an index of traditional orientation. To many settlers on the island the 'power of the Church' appears as an obstacle to progress towards modernity. Those who grumble about the restrictions placed on Sunday activities cite anecdotal evidence of what they see as hypocritical attitudes. These tales have an apocryphal quality. In one example a minister is said to have called for the Department of Agriculture officer to give artificial insemination to his cow one Sunday. But because it was the Sabbath the minister refused to pay and the officer had to make a return trip of fifty miles on Monday. In another narrative a taxi-driver told of frequent trips to the country on Sundays. He had to take beer and whisky from Stornoway to a group of men who waited for these provisions hiding in a garage. It is only possible to purchase alcohol with a meal on Sundays, and the hotels which provide the service are nearly all in Stornoway. Another story, which was the basis of a local court case, concerns the 'meal' with which alcohol was served in one hotel. It is reputed to have consisted of a plate of sandwiches which had gathered dust over many weeks of being produced specifically for the Sabbath. A further well-publicised incident occurred in 1977 when the only cinema in the islands was closed down. The reason given by local authority was that the building did not conform to fire regulations. But the closure took place in the middle of a furore over the showing of the film *Jesus Christ Superstar*, which was regarded by some as blasphemous. One local minister was reported to have laid a curse on the cinema manager. The paradox of this story is that in previous months the cinema had shown the explicitly sexual film *Emanuelle*, which had not raised the same outraged reaction from Church leaders.

Even discussing these stories will be offensive to many islanders. The role of religion is a sensitive area, which affects the self-image of the Hebridean. Yet because of its ideological importance it cannot be ignored. Religious experience and ritual have social effects and perform vital social functions within the Hebrides in both protestant and Roman Catholic areas. Nowhere is this more clearly exhibited than in Lewis. Observation of its persuasive influence should not be construed as criticism.

One factor often ignored by critics of the puritan faith in Lewis is the piety with which religious tenets are observed and held. This is as import-ant as the much discussed 'hypocrisy'. I found it easy to appreciate as I listened to two elderly women discussing the delights of their faith during a long bus journey. They finally parted with affection, saying that it had given them strength to share their pleasure in Jesus through this accidental meeting. It is also appreciable when grace is said in many houses over the simplest repast, not as an empty ritual but with unaffected sensibility. It is less obvious, but nevertheless present, when a Free Church member asks about a known atheist, 'Does he seem to be a different sort of man? Does he seem to be questioning everything?' It is unusually potent when a min-ister says in the course of an interview, 'It would be good if you came to know Jesus here on Lewis.'

A Lewis Sabbath often appears to be the crux of the Church's influence on the island. Even the seagulls seem muted and the only sanctioned trans-port consists of cars and chartered buses taking the faithful to worship. Yet even middle-aged people can remember a time when 'keeping the Sabbath' was not so rigidly enforced and Sabbath observance arguments not so virulently pursued. The Free Church's open intervention began in this arena in the 1930s. It was not linked to demands for land or to any national political issue. Like current arguments over the opening of leisure centres on Sunday it was of purely local significance. But it is pursued as a matter of universal portent. Then as now the intervention in the political sphere is regarded as necessary because of the sacred trust held by the ministry. To the Free Church the Scripture has a central place in theology. The Bible is an epistemology. The Gaelic word most used to refer to the text is not the phonic Gaelic version of the English 'Bible', but the Gaelic word for 'truth'. All questions can be answered, all problems and disputes settled, by reference to the infallible text. It is an essentially exegetical religion. It is not unusual to hear a sermon in which it is claimed that people should not be misled by 'other statements about the human con-dition' such as science. All we need, the minister claims, is the Bible which is 'the revealed word of God'. The ancient book is the sole reference and justification for all the decisions which can be made in a lifetime.

For many believers communicant membership of one of the presbyterian Churches entails a removal to the sacred sphere. The individual should be so concerned with his salvation that he reduces to a minimum his involve-ment in secular matters. For others the sacred trust of the Scriptures *entails* intervention in political activities. The first major issue in which this group was involved arose in 1935. Until then the MacBrayne mail

steamer across the Minch left Stornoway regularly on Sundays at 11.30 p.m.
The Free Church Presbytery, after asking MacBraynes in vain to stop this
Sabbath-breaking, organised a petition containing 10,000 signatures. Ministers and elders took the petition to island homes to obtain signatures. The
Stornoway Town Council, maybe imagining a high degree of compulsion
to sign under these circumstances, declared the petition unrepresentative.
It was at this point that the Free Church Presbytery seems to have made a
decision to take more interest in the affairs of public bodies. By 1945 there
were two representatives of the Free Church on the Town Council. A
unanimous decision was taken to make further representation to Mac-
Braynes, who had already altered the sailing time to 12.30 a.m. on Monday.

This success set the pattern for future political action and established
Free Church influence in policy decisions. In 1956 a Free Church minister
asked British European Airways to review their plans for Sunday flying.
The airline agreed to be guided by the Town Council who rejected BEA's
plan, thus giving open support to Free Church policies. In 1961 the Free
Church Presbytery of Lewis sent a deputation to the Government, protesting about the proposed NATO base at Stornoway. They argued partly in
terms of the potential danger to the islands in the event of any future war,
but mostly in terms of the religious heritage of Sabbath Observance. They
also gave a warning that Church privileges would be withdrawn from any
Free Church members working in connection with the NATO base. This
threat is tantamount to one of excommunication. The privileges referred
to are not so much access to the sacraments of baptism, marriage and
burial, but the right to be a communicant member of the Church. Withdrawal of this represents the separation of the soul from God. By this
action the Free Church obtained some concessions from the government.
Thus it influenced national and international bodies on the basis of a largely
local issue. Although the NATO base was established, the behaviour of the
men posted there and the extent of Sabbath activities are closely monitored
by Church members and more especially the Lord's Day Observance Society.

Actual Free Church representation on the Stornoway Town Council at
that time was not particularly noticeable. Of the eight Council members
only the Provost was a Free Church man, and he was not a communicant.
There were four men from the Established Church of Scotland, one of
whom admitted to being merely nominal, two unrepresentative episco-
palians and one admitted agnostic. Yet all stated that they took many
decisions with reference to Free Church attitudes. The Free Church, partly
through the medium of the Lord's Day Observance Society, had become an
institutionalised pressure-group. Yet it is interesting to note that it remains
in membership a church of the people. Church of Scotland congregations
are smaller, but it is the denomination of those who can exercise bureaucratic power. The elders of a Church of Scotland congregation in Stornoway
tend to be local councillors, government officers or prominent businessmen.
Some rural villages lack a Church of Scotland church but where one does
exist it will usually be attended by individuals such as the schoolmaster,

district nurse and postmaster, while the majority of villagers flock to the larger Free Church premises.

Members of the Free Church represent or symbolise in themselves the opposition between State and Church by their withdrawal to the sacred sphere. Many oppose vehemently any direct Church representation on public bodies. In part of an *extempore* speech to a packed public meeting a Stornoway shopkeeper expressed this opinion:

There are some people on the Council who have no right to be there in virtue of their occupation . . . The Scriptures from which they preach condemn them from taking part in worldly affairs, yet they are soaked up to the eyebrows in it . . . Theirs is a holy club and the book of rules is the Good Book, the Bible. We call them hypocrites. In the Western Isles people should know more about the Bible and the Scriptures. Advice should come from the pulpit and then people will listen to them.

Applause greeted this speech. But this does not necessarily imply unanimous agreement with the sentiments. Oratory is a highly regarded art in the Hebrides and opposing speeches may be lauded as much for the mode of expression as for the content. There are many public figures, usually men of middle years, whose appearance at a public meeting is almost obligatory because of their acknowledged eloquence.

This speech indicates another feature of Scottish presbyterianism, which has historical roots in the Scottish Reformation. Lay people have a right, even duty, to criticise the actions of ministers. This was the crux of the influence of 'the Men' in the evangelical movement. Newcomers who comment on the religious situation on Lewis often refer to the 'influence of ministers' as if the minister were regarded as an individual who delivers the word of God, one whose pronouncements are infallible. This cannot be the case in the non-episcopalian Churches of Scotland. Only the Bible is regarded as the word of God. But in addition the social situation of a presbyterian minister makes him to some extent accountable to his congregation.

In episcopalian Churches a priest or vicar is sent by his superior in the religious hierarchy to lead a congregation. His role is that of a pastor, a shepherd leading a flock. In the presbyterian situation a minister is 'given the call' to a vacant church by the elders of the congregation. He will almost always be known to the congregation through previous visits to the area and may even have been one of a number of ministers who have preached a trial sermon to the congregation while the position is vacant. His character and preaching ability will be known by reputation and he and his family will have had opportunities to review the area, the congregation and the manse before deciding to 'answer the call'. Minister and congregation are likely to be suited. But the role of the minister is not pastoral. Symbolically removed from the secular sphere, he is socially isolated in many respects. His major concern is the interpretation of the Scriptures and it is the influence of the exegesis of the Bible, rather than the collective power of the ministers, which substantiates the power of religion in Lewis social life.

One minister expressed the difference between his role and that of a Roman Catholic priest by saying: 'The priest tells the people how to vote. We don't do that. If the Bible is their standard they should be able to make the right choice.' But although the minister is a person apart he is a symbol of the sacred sphere to which those committed to Church membership belong. This can lead to a sense of outrage among members of the congregation if a minister takes part in secular activities. The only secular arena in which the elect can be seen to be politically active is the Sabbath question, on which they hold a sacred trust.

The influence of this pressure-group is now taken for granted. In the case of the arrival of the oil-related subsidiary of Fred Olsen Ltd, assurances over Sunday working had to be obtained before the Stornoway Trust agreed to enter into negotiations for a lease on land for the proposed development. The first concrete information about the project was relayed to the people of Lewis at a public meeting called by the developers. The Trust had not then entered into any commitment. An Olsen representative explained to the packed audience in the Town Hall the importance of the proposed development for the economic future of the islands. He implied that a huge industrial complex was envisaged and that the unemployment problems of the area would be virtually solved.

These promises appeared viable in the optimistic atmosphere of the 1973 'Oil Boom'. But Lewismen still asked determined questions about the possibility of Sunday working, and a local industrialist pointed out that his firm had adjusted their schedules to accommodate a six-day working week. Olsen's spokesman stated on this occasion that he could not give a firm assurance that there would be no seven-day working. Commercial pressures might necessitate Sunday work. But long before the lease was signed Olsens had been forced to agree that only essential maintenance would take place on the Sabbath. Despite what was felt as the island's desperate need for industrial development the Trust, mindful of public opinion, was adamant on this point. It is in this respect that the religious community on Lewis feel embattled but maintain a sense of integrity. The observance of Sunday as a day apart from the secular order is often referred to as a religious heritage. But historically speaking it is relatively new. Its strength lies in the unity it imparts. One minister expressed his fear of the superficiality of religion on the mainland, 'Once that comes in it is not religion, it is lost.' He claimed that the Church of Scotland on the mainland would not press for Sabbath observance unless pressured into action by the Free Church or the Free Presbyterian Church. He viewed the country as having reached a 'post-Christian stage' in which Lewis remained 'the last bastion'.

Despite the fact that the Free Church influence on politics is indirect, the significance of religion generally on Hebridean politics is notable. There are three ministers of the Church of Scotland on *Comhairle nan Eilean* as

well as a priest from Benbecula. In 1976, nine of the twenty Lewis councillors were from the Free Church. Two were elders and one the wife of an
elder. Outside the council itself community bodies have been started for
local area politics under a new scheme initiated by the Scottish Council
for Social Service. The communities are often dominated by people who
are important figures in village life: elders, deacons, teachers, people with
office jobs and occasionally ministers of the Church of Scotland. Many
can only be described as outsiders. It is significant also that three *Comhairle
nan Eilean* councillors in 1976 were Englishmen, although none of these
represented Lewis areas.

At the level of local politics the election of representatives seems to
require two qualifications from candidates. The first is often sufficient,
but only the second is usually verbalised. First, candidates should be in
some way outsiders. Thus if their activity as public figures meets with local
criticism this does not damage the fabric of family and neighbourhood
relationships (as in Frankenberg, 1957). Newcomers to a village, such as
mainland or English settlers, are often nominated, so are incoming locals
from other villages or islands who arrive to take up official positions.
Therefore ministers, doctors and teachers are frequently found on local
committees. Where a newcomer is not willing to accept local customs,
criticises agricultural methods or advocates wholesale change, it is unlikely
that he or she will be nominated. Exceptionally, an extraordinary individual may be socially regarded as external enough for nomination. Conceptually these people will be outsiders, not outright nonconformists but
nevertheless singular as people. Such a person might have uncommon personal gifts of wit or oratory and thus be above criticism, or be one who
has already survived criticism and still remained in village life.

The second qualification is ability to deal with the agents of English
bureaucracy and modes of business activity. This makes newcomers particularly likely to be chosen. But local people who are employed in post
offices or banks are also frequently nominated. In this process educational
qualifications and certificates, the marks of success in the English-speaking
external world, carry as much weight as natural political ability.

Thus the most interesting factor in the political life of the Western Isles
is the way in which central government and local politics are conceptualised and institutionalised. Although the islands were deeply involved in the
early development of the British Labour Party, class relationships are now
more likely to be conceptualised through nationalism. Yet the tension
between central government and local life takes two contrasting forms. It
is important for the representative of the Western Isles in Westminster to
be a local man. But it is equally important for representatives in local
government to be outsiders. In the case of the Member of Parliament the
implication that he is the voice of the Hebrides in Westminster might perhaps justify the use of the anthropological term 'broker'. The MP physically
travels between two different worlds. But the necessity for him to be a
local man entails that he is only *at home* on the Western Isles where a good

reputation is necessary to his standing. Islanders will admit that the MP
has 'two lives, one here and one in Westminster'. But the life of the islands
is primary. The MP for the Western Isles does not have one foot in each
world. He belongs to the Western Isles and is delegated to go to Westminster.

For different reasons representatives on local committees and councils
cannot be regarded as 'brokers'. They are nominated for office because
they have certain talents which can be put to use in the service of local
interests. Their election is a strategy on the part of the electorate, which
has little to do with a brokerage in which the ways of the outside community are mediated for a peasant Community. There is a general awareness in the islands of the way in which the outside world operates. It is not
their way but it has to be dealt with, and they choose the most appropriate
agents for this task.

6

My people; my village; my home

The academic genre of Community Studies has always placed great emphasis on the ties of kinship. The face-to-face interaction of village life is contrasted with the contractual and single-stranded relationships of urban existence. It cannot be denied that the biological and social ties of parent and child, brother and sister, man and woman are the most immediate experienced by human beings. It is not difficult to see why kinship theory has become dominant in the anthropology of small groups such as hunting and gathering bands. But the emphasis placed on kinship network in rural areas of Western societies often appears to be reliant upon the myth of pre-industrial Community discussed in Chapter 1. It depends upon the moral evaluation of a notion of family and often implies a richer quality of relationship, of closeness, than that experienced in cities.

There are some aspects of Hebridean life which might be taken to confirm this moral notion. But it will not be claimed here that the quality of interpersonal relationships is richer in the Western Isles than it is in urban centres. There are differences between the two areas, but they should not be subjected to ethical judgements. In every human society the experience of the person, learning and increasing knowledge of face-to-face relationships, progressing through the biological cycle of growth and decay, are marked socially. It provides the most important accumulation of knowledge in the life of any individual and has given to anthropology the bulk of its subject matter. In this study of the Western Isles the major interest is in the changes which operate in larger social arenas than the individual life-cycle. But individuals nestle in the interstices of these changes and often appear to experience their own life changes without much reference to the revolutions and social mutations of which they are an organic part. Kinship provides an explanation of behaviour at this psychologically important level. Although it cannot be ignored in any description of the Western Isles, it should not be over-emphasised. The 'criss-crossing ties of kinship' which Arensberg and Kimball described as being the 'raw material of community life' (Arensberg & Kimball, 1940, p. 125) should not be placed in a false opposition to industrial society.

The description of Hebridean family and neighbourhood relationships which will be attempted here should be read as an account taken from observations made in the ethnographic present of 1975—6. It is included to illustrate the cultural specificity of the Western Isles. In describing changes as part of the development of capitalist relationships in the United

Kingdom it has not been the intention to deny the unique social aspects of the area.

Even the language of rural family life in the Western Isles differs from that of most of the United Kingdom. It is Gaelic, often referred to as the language of the Garden of Eden, which is spoken in the home context. The status of this ancient tongue is curious. Unlike Welsh, to which it is related as one of the Celtic group of languages, it is not an official language of the European Economic Community. Despite the bardic tradition, its use as a language of literacy declined sharply in the years following the break-up of the clan system. For a long period after this, Gaelic was rigorously suppressed by educational authority. Islanders of middle years can recall this policy from their school days. Rural children whose mother tongue was Gaelic found it difficult to adjust to the compulsory use of English at all times in the Stornoway secondary school. This increased the feelings of dislocation caused by having to live in hostels in the town during the week, and in many cases the psychological effects linger in adult life. There is a frequently expressed feeling that Gaelic has no value as a language, that one should be ashamed to speak it, that it cannot be of any use in getting employment or qualifications.

But with all these disadvantages the language has continued to be the chosen medium of expression in rural areas. In the more remote villages it is not uncommon for children to speak little or no English until they enter school at the age of five. English is the language of literacy and activities external to the home. Thus the form of English spoken tends to be elaborate, related to the written context in which it is first encountered. Gaelic remains an oral rather than literate mode of communication. People tend to speak Gaelic in the house but write letters home in English. This has effects on the range of vocabulary. The two languages are maintained as distinctive meaning systems because of the practical separation of the contexts in which they are learned and used. This does not just imply two systems of words but can also entail a dual referential system. Children

learned English in the school context only, and this was done mainly through reading books. Since these books were frequently illustrated, however inadequately, the illustrations often provided symbols for the language being learned. A word e.g. 'church' would be associated with what was being read and seen. If a story dealt with, for example, a priest dressed in a cassock reading from his prayer book, and an adjacent illustration showed a church with its spire and bell-tower, these aspects would become associated with each other and with the word 'church'. Whereas '*eaglais*' (church) was learned in the home context and the associations were very different: instead of the priest in his cassock there was the minister in his car, instead of the prayer book there was 'divine inspiration', and instead of the bell-tower and spire there was nothing. The stories and illustrations in books may have become referents in themselves and not merely symbols: the world which they symbolised being virtually unknown (Macleod, 1966, p. 32).

The two semantic worlds of bilingualism can be thought of as present-ing an interesting problem for kinship theory. The kin terminology of Gaelic differs in its classificatory structure from that of English. Gaelic, for instance, makes a terminological distinction between mother's brother (*brathair mo mhathair*) and father's brother (*brathair m'athair*). This cor-responds to a difference in attitude to maternal and paternal kin. *Taobh mo'mhathair* are the people on my mother's side which contrasts with *taobh m'athair*, the people on my father's side. As one Gaelic speaker stated: 'Of course we distinguish between the two, its absolutely differ-ent. It's known that each single line is different. And it's perfectly true. *Tha e anns na daoine* (It's in the people) and whatever it is comes out in a person today.'

Any reference to 'my people' usually refers to the paternal line as might be expected, for patronymics are the mode of Gaelic appellation. But there is an ethos of warmth towards maternal kin. Although the actual operation of kin relationships depends to a large extent on personality there is supposed to be a particular attachment between maternal uncle and nephew. But the obligations which are reported to have previously been due to specific degrees of relationship are now forgotten. Even the conceptual distinction between maternal and paternal kin is disappearing as children reared in an increasingly English environment now translate the English 'my uncle' back into Gaelic as *'m'uncail'*.

Older people are still vitally aware of kinship links and will trace genea-logical relationships vertically and horizontally. This will be done to estab-lish links on occasions where a member of one village marries a stranger from a different part of the islands or a mainlander with Hebridean ancestry. It is also used to establish a potential face-to-face relationship with visitors or to place someone of whom there is no knowledge by acquaintance.

The usual mode of doing business is on a personal basis between people who are known to each other. Kin and neighbourhood links are maintained in the Western Isles over long distances. Thus people in a remote village can see the photograph of a wedding in the local newspaper and locate the couple by relating them to individuals they already know or know of. This faculty is stronger in older people who may be turned to for advice in tracing these relationships. The *Stornoway Gazette* is much used for this purpose and in rural households may be read and re-read throughout the week until the print is almost illegible on the crumpled pages. The indivi-duals named in the paper can be placed as 'the girl from Lewis that John Angus's nephew married' or 'the auntie of the schoolteacher who was down here a while back'.

This system has its advantages. The Council surveyor who comes to do a confidential survey for the new clinic is John Murdo, whose antecedents can be traced, and who is therefore particularly welcome to a cup of tea. In this way a good deal of official information is disseminated by hearsay, knowledge which in an urban setting might appear secret and withheld from inhabitants. Once beyond the Hebrides the system becomes stretched

beyond the stage at which it can be useful. Many country-dwellers find it
difficult to carry out business transactions in any other mode. Thus when
they are unable to make personal contact with individuals in a body such
as the Highlands and Islands Development Board the transaction becomes
meaningless for them. The Board, in Inverness, is frequently described as
'too far away' to be of any practical consequence. Some areas lack the
presence of an articulate group with the ability to manipulate external
bureaucracy. The few individuals in any one village who possess this faculty,
like the school-teacher and district nurse, may lack the numerical strength
which would render their activity effective. In this way the egalitarian
ethos of island life works to prevent the political efficacy of the inhabitants of more remote areas.

Egalitarianism is often overtly expressed in terms of address. Prefixes
like Mr or Mrs are seldom used even in the work situation. Individuals are
referred to and addressed by their Christian name or names, or particularly
by a nickname. The range of surnames in the islands is small. It is effectively
minimised because certain names are confined to particular areas. Thus
Scalpay has many MacSweens and Ness a large proportion of MacIvers.
There is a similar restriction in Christian names. This arises partly from the
habit of naming children after grandparents. There is a felt obligation to
do this, especially in the case of a first grandchild. Thus the first boy will
be named Angus James for his two grandfathers, Angus and James. If male
grandchildren are not born, a girl may be called by the female form of her
grandfather's name, Angusina for instance. There are cases of boys being
named for grandmothers who lack a granddaughter. Young parents do rebel
against this obligation. Occasionally a more modern or anglicised version of
a name will be used. Thus baby Joanna will be named for her grandmother,
Joan. But older people deplore this.

When grandparents have at least one child named for them the parents
are free to name a new infant after an aunt or uncle. Alternatively a fresh
name altogether may be chosen, very occasionally even currently popular
'English' names like Samantha or Jason. But it is even more common to
find one or more siblings or several cousins named for the same grand-
parent. Thus one may find three brothers called Donald, although the second name is usually added to avoid confusion. Thus they will be known
as Donald, Donald Alec and Donald John.

It is not surprising that nicknames are much in use. But what appears to
the outsider as a profusion of ways of naming can be better regarded as
one of the functions of bilingualism. To Gaelic-speakers the formal English
name can seem to have little relevance to the concept of self. The anglicised
version of names bears little phonic relationship to their Gaelic form.
Aonghas Domhnallach sounds very different from Angus Macdonald.
Tormod is not much like Norman, *Ealasaid* like Elisabeth, nor *Seonaid* like
Janet. The Gaelic mode of address via a patronymic, with the prefixes *Mac*
(son of) and *Nic* (daughter of) do not correspond to the use of patrilineal
family surnames in English. When English was first used in an official

bureaucratic context in predominantly Gaelic-speaking areas this caused difficulties. English-speaking bureaucrats could not spell Gaelic names. Gaelic-speakers might not know the English equivalents of their names, equivalents which did not sound or look like the names by which they had been known to others and to themselves throughout their lives. There is a tradition that many men fought the whole of the First World War under a false English name or that of a brother or cousin. To verify this myth would be spurious; it illustrates the separation of the two contexts of Gaelic/ English bilingualism.

There are roughly five different modes of address in use. The given name itself, usually in English, can be used with or without the surname. Thus a woman may be referred to or called Catriona, Catriona Macleod or the diminutive Kathy or Trina. Where there is more than one possible shortened form they may all be used for the same person. Often a second Christian name is used to help identify an individual. But as the class of names in use is relatively small, it can be difficult for an outsider to discover exactly which Kathy or Donald Alec is being discussed. Such identification skills depend on the extent of one's knowledge of interrelationships, and social context.

In Gaelic, a patronymic is the most common way of referring to an individual. Thus *Dhomhnuill Allen* is Donald son of Alan. *Mac* and *Nic* are often omitted. Nicknames are occasionally included in patronymics alongside proper names. Where a mother is a strong personality or has brought up children on her own, her name can be used rather than that of her husband. It is she who is remembered in the genealogy, as she was the important social personality. Thus *Coinneach Kate* will be Kenneth son of the well-known character Kate. This form of appellation can also be an indication of illegitimacy.

A further common Gaelic usage is the prefix *bean*, or 'wife of'. It places the woman, but the man is given by his position not his relationship. *Bean Calum* is thus the wife of Malcolm, who may not be referred to by her own given name even when widowed. Paradoxically a wife reverts to her maiden name on death. The surname used on her coffin is that of 'her people' even though she will be buried alongside her husband in the burial ground of 'his people'. Catherine Macdonald can marry Norman Macleod and be known officially as Catherine Macleod, or in Gaelic as *bean Tormod*, throughout her married life. But it is never forgotten that she is Catherine Macdonald. She will be referred to as such in life by friends and relatives, in death on her coffin and on her gravestone.

The most universal form of appellation is by a nickname. There seem to be two forms of origin. One type arises in the family context in early childhood. It is usually meaningless and can be derived from a baby's mispronunciation of his given name or of some other word. Unlike English names of this sort, which are rapidly enshrined in maternal lore, the origin of a particular name is usually forgotten. In English social life such baby names tend not to persist in adult life nor to be used beyond the immediate family circle. If they do they can be a source of embarrassment. In the Western Isles they can be retained through life and even used in patronymics.

The second most usual source of nickname is the peer group. Such names usually arise in youth due to some individual characteristic. Thus a boy who is good at football might be called Tackle. These names are not always descriptive of character or personal traits. Some refer to an event, and may be difficult to trace to their origin. Examples of peer-group names exist in English and Gaelic. It adds a flavour of comradeship and character to conversation when individuals are referred to as Bill Fling, the Pope, Critical Dan or Harris Tweed.

Within a village the proper English version of a person's name may be only half-remembered. Croft houses rarely bear numbers or names. Often it is only the postman who will know the 'correct' names and addresses of inhabitants. To live successfully in a village one has to use a set of knowledges about other inhabitants which differs entirely from the way official agencies name them or locate their homes. This can present some difficulties for outsiders like officials from the Department of Agriculture and Fisheries. One cannot stop the car in the middle of a straggling crofting settlement and ask a passer-by for directions to 'Donald Macaulay at Number 12' with any certainty of success. One needs to know Donald Macaulay's nickname and some personal characteristics. It is easier to find someone described as 'a big fellow with a beard' in a village of 500 inhabitants where beards are uncommon, than to find Donald Macaulay at Number 12. Proper names are so rarely in use that the area of Ness in Lewis has produced its own telephone directory listing subscribers by their nicknames.

Throughout the islands large families are widely regarded as the norm. This is as true of the protestant north as of the Roman Catholic south. Family size in the Hebrides is significantly larger than the United Kingdom average. District nurses do not report any particular ignorance of, or resistance to, contraceptive methods except on religious grounds in Roman Catholic areas. But the ideology of marriage entails procreation. A young couple is expected to produce a child within only a few years of marriage. A young man can be teased by his workmates until his wife is pregnant. The expectation is that the couple should have a child for the rest of the family. 'The family will be thinking they have had to wait', is typical of remarks made of a couple expecting a baby after four years of marriage. Women will state with pride that they 'have five of a family' meaning five children. To have only one child is regarded as a misfortune and unfair to the child who is expected to be lonely. To be childless is to be an anomaly, more strongly felt in the Hebrides than in urban areas. In most human societies there is no possibility for a childless woman to be admitted to the total sphere of female activity and conversation. In the Hebrides there are few career opportunities for women and little perception of the possibility of a female role which is not tied to the domestic sphere. One woman sobbed when told that she could never have children. 'But how will I pass the time?' It is not unknown for a childless couple to informally adopt one of the younger offspring of their more fertile siblings.

The concept of family can in any case be regarded as open-ended. This is particularly visible in the care of young children which is the task of household, family and close neighbours. When a pre-school-age child is in the room it is the sole object of conversation and the focus of attention. Both men and women pet and fondle babies constantly. One rarely hears a child crying for attention. Older girls seem to enjoy taking charge of small children. Although this is usually the task of older girls they learn the responsibility early. It is not unusual to see a five-year-old staggering under the weight of an eighteen-month-old brother whom she has taken from his cot to calm his tears. This is not done to play at being adult but is part of the learned role of the child. Older girls will call at a neighbour's house to ask if they can take the baby for a walk. Looking after young children is viewed as a privilege and one is not aware of young siblings following older brothers or sisters as unwelcome additions to a group. Teasing and even bullying take place in school situations where children from different villages mix. But within the village, perhaps because the number of available playmates is often small, playgroups are vertical in terms of age and there seems to be very little serious quarrelling.

The village and surrounding countryside is the children's play environment. It is in this sphere, external to individual homes, that they meet and form social relationships once they have reached school age. Most houses in the village will be open to them, but there is no formal visiting pattern, no idea of having a friend to tea after school. Once a child has reached school age the constant fondling attention from adults ceases abruptly. The children become part of the society of village children which is their reference group out of school hours.

This does not mean that personal contact with adults ceases but there is a sharp separation between the role of baby and that of school child. Besides learning a social role among its peers in the village the child has to acquire an appropriate set of family roles and responsibilities. Sex-linked roles are learned early. In some crofting households fathers are at home for much of the week engaged in agriculture, weaving or fishing. If the father is not home there is usually an uncle or neighbour engaged in these tasks. Boys naturally take part in these activities as part of their education in crofting. It is this association of boys with men which develops consciousness of the male role rather than any verbal reiteration of male qualities.

Girls likewise follow the pattern of their mothers' activities and are thus effectively confined to the village and its immediate vicinity except during peat cutting when whole families take part. This can lead to a separation of spacial and geographical knowledge. In one village it was discovered that female knowledge only extends to the boundaries of the infield. Beyond that, on the moor, women and girls are without bearings and quite lost. Boys, however, learn the paths across the moor, the names of features and the best places for fishing. In this way male and female knowledge is separated not through initiation but through association.

In this particular fishing community it would have been anthropologically interesting to have found that the pier and harbour were regarded as symbolically prohibited for women. This has been found to be the case in other North Atlantic fishing communities. Yet it did not seem that there were any specific spacially demarcated male and female areas in the Hebrides. On the other hand, women were seldom seen on the fishing-jetty and did not think of going on board a fishing-boat except occasionally for a pleasure trip or coastal transport. The notion of women going fishing tended to be treated with astonishment, rather than any fear that they would bring bad luck to boat and catch. It was believed that women would look foolish in fishing gear. Women in remoter rural areas do not wear trousers even when cutting peat or herding sheep. Moreover, it is commonly regarded as natural for women to stay at home and have children. Comments in essays by rural secondary school children reflect this distinction: 'Men cannot make children's food or do the beds'; 'Women who go to work do not get the same pay as men because their employers know that a woman should be rightly at home'; 'Women do not have the physical strength to stand up to a whole day's work, except when she is doing housework.'

These opinions are given despite the anomalies which exist in many villages. Because young women often leave the island permanently to work on the mainland there is frequently a surplus of bachelors in any one village. It is not uncommon for men to keep house very efficiently for themselves, cleaning and cooking as well as any local woman. Bachelor sons also often tend and nurse elderly parents. In addition there is no bar to education for girls. If a girl is discovered to be talented at school she will be encouraged to take further education as if she were a boy. One of the strongest drives in Hebridean family life is the search for educational qualifications which are the passport to secure adult employment.

There is a latent antagonism between the sexes, particularly in rural areas. This must be partly due to the ideological separation of roles. But the practical separation of activities from an early age makes male/female friendship uncommon because of the lack of a common context. Thus the closest relationships between the sexes occur in the household context between siblings. Occasionally this applies to first cousins also, particularly if neighbourhood ties strengthen those of kinship. Other than this, friendships tend to arise between members of the same sex. There are variations throughout the islands, but even in Stornoway there is an atmosphere of competitive antagonism between young men and women which is expressed in verbal exchange. It is frequently stated that a young man has to 'take a drink' to gain the courage to approach a young woman.

Once a couple are known to be courting, their roles and behaviour change. But open affection between courting, engaged or married couples is rare, especially in the country. In over three months spent in one fishing village I did not make a single observation of a couple going about together except in cars. Women often showed affection towards each other when walking through the village. Mother and daughter, sisters and female friends frequently walk arm-in-arm. Women generally have a physical closeness with other women which is expressed in body contact; an arm around the shoulders or simply standing much more closely together than would be the norm in many other parts of Britain. In one fishing village, the only mixed-sex couples seen together were men with elderly mothers. Bachelor sons living at home often went shopping and carried the bags for their mothers. In the general case, men would only shop in this village for specific items such as newspapers, cigarettes or fishing equipment. Married couples were usually only seen out together in cars, although they might make joint visits on formal occasions. Most visits were made independently and women in this village complained that their husbands often would not even accompany them to a wedding. This should not be taken to imply that close companionship does not exist between married couples. But it tends to be a companionship based only on the shared context of the home. The conjugal bond is regarded as the source of practical rather than psychological satisfactions.

As the relationship between siblings is strong, aunts and uncles, particularly if they are unmarried, are important child-rearing agents. They take a constant personal interest in the welfare of nieces and nephews. Aunts often visit with a gift of new clothing. The nature of such gift will not necessarily be discussed beforehand. They will know from their intimate acquaintance with the child what is needed and what will be deemed suitable.

There is in any case only a relatively small range of clothing styles available in the islands. This, together with the desire of people in smaller communities not to arouse comments about their appearance, leads to a certain conformity in modes of apparel. There are some conventions in dress which are clearly discernible. As stated above women in rural areas tend not to wear trousers. In Lewis the ministers are said to frown on the practice. One young man told of the case of his aunt, who had severe rheumatism in her knees and who wished to keep her legs warm by wearing trousers. Despite the fact that she wore a skirt over the trousers in order to maintain propriety she still incurred the censure of her minister.

Dark colours are preferred by older women in rural areas particularly for individuals who have entered full Church membership. Black is prescribed for widows. Most older women wear their hair in a tight bun at the back of the neck, scorning adornment and the use of cosmetics. In any case the more-or-less constant wind and rain make elaborate hairstyles and make-up difficult to maintain. It is easier to opt for the all-purpose headscarf, which many women wear all day long, even in the house. A typical Hebridean housewife will wear a jumper and skirt, headscarf and nylon overall for most of her working day. Because she often has to perform

minor outdoor tasks she needs stout shoes or wellington boots. The mode
of dress in rural areas is determined by the environment and daily tasks
rather than any expression of individual personality.

It is interesting to take a morning bus ride from a rural area into Stornoway. At the furthest point of the route the women who get on the bus will
be dressed in sober shades, their faces lacking make-up and none will be
wearing trousers. As the bus approaches Stornoway the style of dress of
new passengers alters with each village. The colours become brighter, hairstyles more elaborate, lipstick, eyeshadow and trousers all appear in greater
abundance. When the bus returns in the evening it carries a number of
younger women returning from work. They are dressed in the style of their
contemporaries throughout the United Kingdom. Some alight at each village along the route. They are not out of touch with recent trends in music,
dress or taste, nor are their innovations generally disapproved of by older
women.

Men also appear to have a uniform costume of nylon boiler-suit and
woolly hat or flat cap for working tasks. These hats and the thick socks
worn with wellington boots are the only items of clothing in everyday use
which are regularly made with the wool used for Harris Tweed. Tourists
and newcomers wear tweed coats. Crofters sometimes wear tweed jackets
when they attend local sheep and cattle markets. But the most common
outdoor wear for local people of all ages is the hooded waterproof anorak
or kagool.

On evening visits and official occasions more formal wear is adopted.
But Sunday apparel is noticeably different from that of secular days. It
can be difficult to recognise one's crofter neighbour in the sober-suited,
black-hatted churchgoer. The housewife abandons her scarf and dons a
smart hat, expensive coat and lightweight shoes. In Lewis the style is
sober, but in one Harris village the women's Sunday hats tend to have
large, filmy, floppy brims and are difficult and unsuitable for wearing in
high winds.

As Harris Tweed tends to be the choice of outsiders rather than locals,
so another of the casual visitor's expectations is confounded. Tartans and
kilts are seldom worn, even on ceremonial occasions. There is scant historical evidence for their use in the Hebrides. Early accounts of island dress
describe the garb common in the Highlands, known as fillibeg and plaid,
which has been dated back to at least 1099 (Goodrich-Freer, 1902, p. 275).
The fillibeg was a large piece of rough woollen cloth wound around a man's
waist and through his legs to cover his shoulders and head as a cape. At
night it could be rewound as a blanket to sleep in.

Buchannan described the men of the Hebrides in the late eighteenth century as wearing

the feilabeg, and the short hose, with bonnets sewed with black ribbons
around their rims and a slit behind with the same ribbon in a knot. Their
coats are commonly tartan, striped with black, red or some other colour,

after a pattern made, upon a stick of the yarn, by themselves, or some other ingenious contriver. Their waistcoats are either of the same or some such stuff; but the feilabegs are commonly of breachan, or fine Stirling plaids, if their money can afford them (Buchannan, 1793, pp. 84–5).

This was clearly the apparel on formal occasions, for Buchannan states that for common work the men wore 'short or long coats and breeches made of striped cloth' and wool shirts (ibid, p. 85). Women could be seen in striped or tartan gowns with married women wearing a linen mutch or cap (ibid, p. 87).

Nineteenth-century accounts echo this picture. But they do not mention tartan as the garb of the people, despite the fact that it had by then become a popular pattern for aristocratic wear as part of the cult of Highlandness or Balmoralism espoused by Queen Victoria. One visitor to the Western Isles described the people as wearing clothes of their own manufacture, with hardly any linen or cotton in use. The women wore striped or coloured clothes, the men brown or grey (Mitchell, 1883, 1971, p. 233). A nineteenth-century resident described the colours used as principally the natural white and grey of wool with the addition of crotal, a dye from moss, which produced a dark, brown colour. Indigo blue was used to dye the jacket and trousers of fishermen and the outer petticoats of women (Smith, 1875, pp. 60–4).

The general impression is that clothing of rural people in the nineteenth century did not differ greatly from that worn by the herring girls and coopers shown in Plate 5. The change in style since then has been accompanied by a change from woollen fabric to synthetic fibres. One of the paradoxes of islands famous for the production of a natural cloth is the proportion of acrylic and nylon textiles chosen by the islanders. There are several contributing factors. First there is the consideration of cost. Clothes made in synthetic fibres tend to be cheaper. But for many islanders Harris Tweed seems to be old-fashioned despite its warmth and hard-wearing qualities. Synthetic fibres have the added advantage of being easy to wash and dry especially when a washing machine is used. This is a vital factor determining choice of fabric for clothing and household use in the inclement climate of the Hebrides.

Although aunts and uncles buy clothes for children it is seldom that they purchase toys. Manufactured playthings are not a major feature in Hebridean childhood. Learning through play is achieved in real rather than surrogate situations. Little girls do have 'dollies' but there is more fulfilment to be gained in the care of a younger brother or a neighbour's child. Boys, like their contemporaries throughout Europe, are obsessed with football. But who will play at 'cops and robbers' when there is a chance to join a fishing expedition?

One more recent pastime of old and young alike provides a set of cultural assumptions which the people of the Western Isles share with those of the rest of Britain. Watching television has become a common activity in many homes. Until 1976 the islands enjoyed poor reception of only one television channel. They could view simply the lighter programmes of the British Broadcasting Corporation. Now that new reception masts have been provided it is possible for people in some areas to watch in colour and to receive the more 'highbrow' BBC2 as well as that of the commercial Independent Television Authority. Regionally oriented programmes are available and there is some broadcasting in Gaelic but the bulk of programmes is the same as that provided for the national viewing public. Presbyterian influences disapprove of television, especially on the Sabbath, but the medium provides a set of cultural values and assumptions which cannot help but influence attitudes and tastes. On my last evening in one village I paid a visit to each of the houses where I was well known in order to make my farewells. It was a Wednesday. Usually the narrow village streets would have been busy with young people walking about in single-sex groups engaged in verbal exchange or with older people paying visits to neighbours. But it was as silent as a Sabbath. I could not understand this absence of people. Even the shops, which were usually open until 10 p.m. had apparently closed for the evening. I began to feel that I had unaccountably missed the date of some religious observance or not been informed of the death of a villager. But the answer lay in the fact that almost the entire population was watching the heavyweight championship fight between Muhammed Ali and Joe Frazier on television.

Television will presumably change some Hebridean attitudes towards entertainment. One fundamental consequence could be in Gaelic literature. Bardic tradition and Biblical exegesis alike have led to a tendency towards non-fiction. There are legends, folk-tales and ghost stories, but these gain their effectiveness from an apparent factual base and often give a mythical source for the existence of a specific feature of the landscape or the origin of a particular family. One local author claimed that the Gael has no sense of fiction. He mentioned a fictional story he had written which described the death of an old man. An elderly neighbour had questioned the author closely to find out if the man described had been the author's father. A negative response had brought forth the question 'Was it your uncle then?' When the author attempted to explain that the character was a fictional creation his neighbour had failed to understand and replied 'Well, it must be your cousin then.'

Plays and films have never been plentiful on the islands. Television is the first universally available medium for fictional entertainment. Through news and documentary programmes, television also disseminates information and attitudes which include the Hebrides in a manufactured form of British national heritage. It should not be forgotten that the Hebridean component of this heritage is a reiteration of the view of the islands as backward, traditional and quaint. The Western Isles are represented to the United Kingdom and to themselves as beautiful, remote and removed from urban pressures. It is seldom that the islands' economic and social problems receive either informed or serious media treatment.

The long-term effects of television on island life are difficult to predict and in any case sociological understanding of the effects of mass media is a matter for debate. One frequently-expressed popular opinion is that television has stopped people from providing their own entertainment. It is hard to assess the veracity of this claim in terms of a direct cause and effect and it seems probable that there is more than one factor at work in the apparent decline of home- or family-based recreational activities. But it is clearly the case that in the Hebrides the ceilidh has undergone transformation.

As enshrined in Hebridean folk-memory a ceilidh was an evening gathering in one of the village houses at which stories would be told and songs sung. The atmosphere tended to be informal but would resemble a party if there was occasion for celebration. One elderly islander remembered:

Looking back, it was a great life and a great social life as well. As children we used to sit and listen to the old tales the *cailleachs* (old women) told. Mostly they were stories of days gone by, their experiences. Some of them were great storytellers too. A lot of the stories were about ghosts and things. It had a purpose. We used to go out at night and it was to keep us out of mischief, to scare us and to keep us inside at night.

The most frequent place of rendezvous would be the house of some person, usually a man and often a bachelor, who had a reputation for being a good host and storyteller. In one village I was shown the ruins of one such ceilidh house which had reputedly burnt down after a particularly notable revel. Significantly, the ruin was that of a *tigh dubh*, or black house, an important component of memories of the way things used to be.

The black house of the Hebrides is often described as the traditional home of the area. It was a single-storey building with thick stone walls and a thatched roof (Figure 3). The name *tigh dubh* is not particularly ancient, but appeared in the nineteenth century to distinguish the older type of housing from the new 'white houses' which proprietors and State agencies encouraged for reasons of health and hygiene. In the opinion of these authorities the simple *tigh dubh* sheltering humans and animals alike, lacking light and ventilation, was insanitary. But the low stone building was an efficient refuge from the harsh winds, and merged with the landscape of which it appeared to be an integral and natural feature. Because there were few internal partitions the *tigh dubh* contributed a spatial sense of family in which the generations shared their daily lives (Fenton, 1978).

The family assembly in a black house in the evening, when friends and neighbours dropped in, was the cultural source of the ceilidh tradition. Occupancy of black houses continued until well into this century. Some are now used as barns and beside many a modern Hebridean dwelling, the stout walls of the black house which sheltered a previous generation stand as a permanent reminder of the recent past. Memories of the social life they symbolise linger in speech and literature. In a school essay, written in 1964, a Lewis girl described the ceilidh atmosphere.

Section through twentieth-century black house

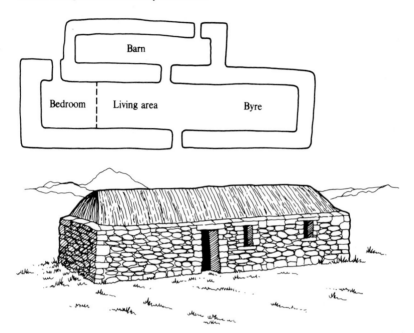

Figure 3. The *tigh dubh* or black house. (*Sources*: Thompson, 1968, p. 67; Fenton, 1978, p. 10.)

During winter, many neighbours come in each night. We form a circle round the fire and discuss many subjects. The fire can be built as high as you like because there is no risk of a chimney catching fire.

Very often, after tea a *cailleach* comes in for a *ceilidh*. You know just to gossip. I remember a few years ago, when my uncle was at home from Canada, people used to come every night. What times we had singing . . .

The black house is definitely the cosiest you can find.
(*West Side Story*, Shawbost School, May 1964).

'Ceilidh' now has a variety of uncertain meanings. Posters in Stornoway advertise a 'ceilidh and dance' in a local hotel with a professional band. People will say 'come over tonight and we'll have a ceilidh'. But this tends to signify a semi-formal visit rather than an evening of story-telling and songs. On such an occasion the atmosphere will be relaxed, drinks and refreshments will be served and discussion and enjoyment may last till the early hours of the morning. There will be no watching television, for the visit will be an occasion for the host to concentrate on guests and extend warm hospitality. But a ceilidh can also be spontaneous. Thus a man might explain a hangover to his friend at work by saying 'Calum came to show me his new car, and we had quite a ceilidh.'

Some ceilidhs resemble the occasions enshrined in popular memory. In 1976 a group of Canadian Eskimos made an official visit to the Hebrides as part of a tour of Scotland in which they were examining questions of land rights. A ceilidh which included singing and dancing was organised in their honour in Stornoway and the Eskimos delighted their hosts by contributing some of their own songs and dances. Yet a poem written by a Lewis man to record the event expresses the sensation that this was a temporary resurgence of things past and now in decay. The situation of the colonised Eskimos appears as a metaphor for the Hebridean condition.

Strange Meeting

Ten Eskimos came
     to the Isle of Lewis
Grave were they
     as we ourselves
We sang
   to them songs
Of love and parting
     silent they sat
And did not smile
    Music we played
They tapped their feet
     Tapped their feet
To the Gaelic beat
    'Sing, Sing,'
We cried
   'Only in Church
Not at home'
    They replied.
Then one got up
     'I'll dance for you
a little number'
    He did too
A Russian dance
    whilst taking off
His anorak
   (just another word
we stole)
    Back and forth
Heel and toe
   'The jacket's off!'
We clap as daft
    to see at last
Some pathetic relic
    of a butchered past.
(Macdonald, 1976).

At times ceilidhs resembling the remembered form take place in island homes. But it seems as if there is a realisation that opportunities for enjoying such occasions are slipping away. In one case I discovered that people were taking cassette tape recorders along to record the singing. It appeared to signify that such ceilidhs were rare and should be preserved.

This is also shown in academic interest in the Hebrides. Bodies such as the School of Scottish Studies collect folktales and songs for research purposes. But the documentation of such testimonies is principally an historical undertaking and tends to concentrate upon recording the rare and unusual historical vestige at the expense of the dynamic present. At a ceilidh organised in Edinburgh by one such academic body some elderly Highlanders came to the evening gathering of a history conference. They joined the participants at the conference in singing songs and telling stories. These men were announced in conference programmes as 'tradition bearers'. Many of those present contributed to the enjoyment, including some English people who sang southern folk-songs. But it seemed as if the 'tradition bearers', respected and popular as they obviously were, appeared as artefacts bearing witness to the myth of a past Community.

One of the normative evaluations of Community states that sharing and mutual help decline in urban or modern situations. It would be difficult to establish the validity of such an opinion except by longitudinal study. But it can be noted that living in a Hebridean village entails being involved in a set of relationships which transcends the boundaries of individual households. One more formal aspect of this is the regulation of common grazings and peat banks, a task which is in the control of a village grazings clerk. Certain activities like sheep-dipping and potato-planting tend to be performed on a communal basis. But the size and composition of the groups taking part varies from island to island, and from village to village. Overall historical changes in crofting agricultural practices have already been described. Yet it is difficult to establish a general case for all areas of the Hebrides. The same problem arises when trying to describe patterns of family and neighbourhood visiting. There is a frequently expressed opinion that the atmosphere becomes more friendly the further south in the islands one travels. One Lewisman commented that he felt 'more at home' in Barra and related this to the difference between protestant and Roman Catholic religious values. Each island and each village is reputed for its own general character. Thus the people in one area are reputed to be treacherous, those on the west side of Lewis are supposed to be more friendly than those on the east, the inhabitants of one village are supposed to be witches and Lewis people refer to those on Harris as 'light'.

Two anecdotes from fieldwork can illustrate these differences. One period of research was spent in an area which can only be described as close-knit. The arrival of a stranger was obviously regarded as an interesting event. As I walked through the village with my suitcase I was greeted by passers-by with comments on the weather, 'grand day', even though it was rather overcast. Having settled my few possessions in the house I had rented I walked back to the post office and was greeted by the same individuals, 'You're back then'. Usually it was middle-aged men who spoke. Young men looked away and women only ventured 'hello' or 'good morning' if I smiled at them. Later in the day my next-door neighbour called and without any preliminaries said 'If you want anything you're to ask', following this abrupt welcome with an invitation to visit her home.

News of my arrival and activities were rapidly relayed through the village, principally by shopkeepers who were not slow to question me closely. On subsequent days I was invited into many homes, often by complete strangers whom I met along the road. In the course of a few weeks it was possible to meet and talk to many members of this village where all doors were kept open at all times and no one knocked before entering.

This had its disadvantages for residents. People who were ordered to rest by the doctor were unable to gain peace. If the door was closed visitors would simply knock until it was opened, and illness was one of the most valid reasons for making a visit. During my time in this village one elderly woman had a stroke. She was a popular woman and during her illness her house thronged with well-wishers every evening. The patient was unable to move or speak, yet both the daughter who lived at home and another who flew back from Glasgow were kept busy providing hospitality. 'Some of the visitors', complained another, married, daughter, 'never even got up to see her'.

In another village where I lived for a longer period this intense visiting activity was not so noticeable, nor was a stranger made to feel so welcome. Greetings on the road were perfunctory. The curious questioning of shopkeepers was replaced by a polite but distant attitude. Although rumours abounded, few people ventured to ask what I was doing. Disapproval of the well-known, free-and-easy visiting patterns of the first village was expressed. 'We would never visit a stranger uninvited. But we visit each other as neighbours.' Invitations to visit were less forthcoming and more formal. Yet when January gales brought down the electricity cables and the village was cut off by snow a neighbour, who had never spoken to me before, struggled through the wind and dark to see 'if you have everything you need'. And in terms of close-knit family relationships this village did not differ greatly from the first.

In both villages the attitude towards a stranger was ambivalent but the mode of expression was different. There was help but there was also aggression and the two attitudes would appear in the same individuals, both being part of a protection against the outsider's potentially disruptive, potentially intrusive, presence. In the first village the children of those families where I appeared to be a most welcome visitor would mock and spit at me in the street. In the second I was, like most strangers, subjected to persistent vandalism of my property. One does not need to be English or a mainlander to be a stranger in a Hebridean village. After one particularly dangerous piece of vandalism one villager commiserated with me and offered to informally police my house. He said, 'My mother was a stranger here, so I hate this sort of behaviour to a stranger.' I later discovered that his mother came from a village some twenty miles away.

Village and kinship links are activated in the life-cycle rituals of marriage and burial. Marriage can involve the entire village when it takes place in a rural area. Every household contributes food and most of the women of the village will be involved preparing dishes and decorating the village hall. Young and old inhabitants will be invited to the celebrations and this sometimes necessitates two supper sittings. Music and dancing will carry on throughout the night. In protestant areas a wedding is the only Church-sanctioned occasion for such revelry.

The communal basis for such celebrations is gradually being superseded by more formal wedding receptions in hotels. Similarly, betrothal ceremonies are now replaced by an engagement party and the gift of a ring which is similar to the betrothal pattern of the rest of the United Kingdom. Yet some distinct characteristics remain, showing a mixture of village involvement and hotel-based organisation. One wedding which took place in 1976 shows the pattern which has emerged.

The bride and groom, both in their early twenties, were Lewis born and bred. The groom was from the Point area of Lewis where he shared a council house with siblings, the bride lived on a croft on the west side. They planned to settle in a caravan on this croft after the ceremony. Both had experienced work on the mainland for a spell before returning to jobs on the island. They had known each other since their early teens and had met frequently at dances. The Friday evening dances in village halls and hotels in Stornoway are virtually the only entertainment possibilities for young people. Dances do not usually start until after 10 p.m. and are viewed by many as the cause of over-indulgence in alcoholic refreshment. They are disapproved of by Church authority. The typical dance is a fairly rowdy affair with a live band playing a mixture of pop music and Scottish reels. Even dances held in Stornoway hotels have a friendly, informal atmosphere. Everyone seems to know everyone else and those present are mostly in the eighteen to twenty-four age-group.

The couple had decided to settle on the croft rather than applying for a council house in the groom's village. The bride's parents were getting on in years and she was the youngest of several daughters, all of whom had married and left home. The village, she explained,

has always been my home. Every second house has a relative. Number 6 is my mother's family home. But the way it is now, it's an older generation. Apart from my auntie and cousins I don't go visiting much. As a child I hardly ever passed a house I didn't go in to. But I quite like it apart from the gossips, and now there's another young couple in the village.

When the couple became engaged they had a 'night out and a wee party' with friends. They had decided to get engaged without consulting their parents, who expected it to happen anyway. Rings were chosen on a trip to Inverness. Within three months, arrangements for the wedding were well advanced. The couple had opted for a short engagement, unlike the bride's sisters who had waited for up to seven years between betrothal and marriage. Invitation cards were sent out and presents began to arrive.

Hebridean wedding gifts are lavish and are set out along with the bridal dress for family and friends to view. For about two weeks before the wedding there is a constant stream of visitors in the evening, all looking at the display and all receiving hospitality of tea, sandwiches, cakes and possibly alcoholic drinks. In this particular case the bride's dress was altered from that of her future sister-in-law to save unnecessary expense. 'I had the choice of my sister's or his.' There were to be two bridesmaids, one of the bride's sisters, one of her friends and the groom's small niece as a 'flower girl'. The couple paid all the expenses for dresses, bouquets, buttonholes and the hire of suits for the men. But there are no general conventions as to who bears the expense of any items for the wedding.

The ceremony was arranged with the appropriate minister, mostly by telephone although the couple did go to his house for one formal discussion. In the bride's description of her wedding the service appeared of less interest than the preliminary preparations and the reception. Buses were provided to take the guests from the church to the hotel in Stornoway, two for those from the bride's area, two for those from the groom's home village. The guest list was large and included neighbours and a wide circle of kin, all of whom received formal and informal invitations.

All the organisation for the formal meal was handled by the hotel management. When the guests were at their places the bride and groom proceeded to their place at the top table preceded by a piper. After grace a three-course meal was served. This meal would be the subject of much appraisal and discussion after the event. Hotel weddings are relatively new and the quality of food served by rival establishments is the subject of much interest. If the meal is judged poor it is the hotel rather than the hosts who tend to receive the blame, although it may be stated that the family are 'embarrassed'.

The meal was followed by toasts. All the speeches were in English out of courtesy to non-Gaelic speakers. When the time came for telegrams to be read the best man could not read those in Gaelic. This task was left to a male friend of the bride's family.

The final part of the reception was a dance in the hotel. This began with a Grand March which the bride and groom led around the hall, followed by a bridal waltz. Less formal dancing then continued until the hotel closed just after midnight. The guests dispersed usually to hold informal parties. The bride and groom remained in the hotel overnight and then caught the morning ferry to the mainland for a honeymoon. They 'didn't fancy going to Spain'.

Little of this life-cycle ritual differs from weddings held throughout Britain except in detail. Funerals on the other hand have a characteristic cultural distinctiveness in which there is a remarkable ritual cohesion throughout the Western Isles despite differences in religious persuasion (Vallee, 1955). For an English stranger the importance accorded death and burial often appears oppressive and morbid. Many white settlers object strongly to what Scott described as 'the sacred veneration due to misfortune, which in Scotland seldom demands its tribute in vain' (Scott, 1974, p. 104). There appears to be a dark and brooding side to Hebridean culture which manifests itself in an apparent tendency to dwell upon topics of sudden death and tragedy. This may reflect a genuine statistical trend, for the death rate in the Western Isles is higher than that of the United Kingdom as a whole. This could be a function of the age-structure, and yet from a subjective point of view it appears that there is a higher incidence of tragic and sudden death in the islands. A youth is struck by lightning when returning home from a dance. Another boy disappears on New Year's Eve and his body is discovered in a moorland stream months later. Several fishermen are drowned. A young girl dies as a car in which she is a passenger plunges over a cliff.

Living in the Hebrides one gets the impression that there is an ever-present potential for disaster. Yet this does not indicate that there is a higher incidence of such accidental death. What is remarkable is the extent to which people feel themselves involved in tragedy. This is an indication of the wide range of operative kinship and neighbourhood links in the islands. When death occurs it mobilises a broad set of relationships which implicates a large proportion of the population. There are many people who can, indeed must, claim knowledge of the deceased, who have an obligation to take part in mourning and funeral activities. But it might be claimed that this, or some generalised cultural tendency, leads to that feeling of involvement in the tragic aspects of the human condition which is referred to as 'morbid' by strangers. Sudden death appears as an obsession in the daily newspaper which serves the Highland area. The front page of the *Press and Journal* every Monday features almost exclusively a list of the accidents and injuries which have taken place in the region since Friday night. A plane crash in Eastern Europe will be spoken of in the same conversational tone used to discuss a car crash in a neighbouring village. On a return visit to the islands my first few hours were spent with a fifteen-year-old youth who regaled me with a list of the accidents which had taken place on the island since my last trip.

The exact form taken by mourning and funerals depends upon the area in which death takes place. The urban peoples of Western cultures are now unfamiliar with death and the rituals of mourning. They hand the details over to external professional agents like doctors and funeral directors. Hebrideans have a deep social knowledge of the social processes involved. If there is any sense in which one can talk of the Hebridean Community it is in connection with the respect accorded to death.

When a member of a rural village dies it can effectively halt all activity for as much as a week. Fishermen, on hearing of the death on their radios, will return to the home port until after the funeral. Village shops may close for some portion of the time. Women may not hang out their washing. The looms will be silenced.

News of a village death spreads rapidly, it being the duty of individuals to pass the information on as quickly as possible. If death has occurred during the night the postman often spreads the news when he delivers the morning mail.

The body of the deceased, usually referred to as the 'remains', rests in the family home until the day of the funeral. It lies in an open coffin in the bedroom or occasionally on a table in a sitting-room. Services are held in the house during the evening and these are often led by lay people rather than ministers. The house of the deceased is a centre of activity until late in the evening. Many visitors of all ages come in their best clothes to pay their respects.

What is interesting in this highly religious area is the lay involvement in the ritual and the relatively unimportant role of ministers and priests. It is as if the people wish to retain their relationship with the deceased until the last possible moment. Hebrideans have a strong desire to be buried at home in the plot or 'lair' allocated to their family in the local cemetery. Many of those working on the mainland pay regular sums of money into special funds to cover the expense of returning their bodies home for burial if death should occur. It is a custom which is said to have begun with the herring girls and fishermen who followed the mainland fishing-boats. Burial is the norm and therefore it can be an expensive business to ship bodies from the mainland even though local fishing-boats are sometimes used to transport the remains home across the Minch.

The cemeteries are impressive. They are usually separate from both village and church. Because burial has to take place in sand rather than peat or rock the graveyards are situated close to the sea. The bare grey stones which are used to mark the burial places brazenly outstare the waves breaking on the shore (Plate 14).

Funeral behaviour can be seen anthropologically as a series of ritual separations in which the deceased is gradually detached from the social relationships in which he was involved in life. While the remains lie in the house respect is paid by the widest possible range of social relations. Kin, neighbours and friends old and young are obliged to mark the passing of the individual. The coffin is left open at least for the first night and people occasionally touch the remains on the forehead as they enter the room, particularly if the deceased is a close relation or friend; 'you get some satisfaction from this touch'.

The atmosphere in the evening gatherings is palpably one of mourning and the psalms chosen are appropriate for the occasion. The Bible has a prominent place on the main table in the sitting-room. Psalms and passages from the Bible are read and prayers referring to the deceased and to the situation are composed by both ministers and laymen. Close relatives do not take part. In some areas chairs are brought for mourners from all over the village although it is now the practice to bring them from the school. 'People are crammed all over the house with doors left open. A psalm wafts over the house. The minister prays. Voices come from all over the house in prayers.'

On the day of the funeral the remains are first separated from the

94

Plate 14. A cemetery on the west side of Lewis.

society of women. A short service may be held either in the house, or in a church if the funeral takes place in Stornoway. Then the closed coffin is transported on the shoulders of men either to the cemetery or to the town or village boundary whence it will be transported by hearse to the grave-yard. In this transport from the home to the burial place only men take part. There can be no greater statement of the Hebridean sense of the woman's place within the homestead than this separation. In one village, I saw an elderly woman weeping into her handkerchief as she stood inside her gate. She was watching the coffin, carrying the body of her mother, which was borne on the shoulders of male relatives away out of the village. She stood in the same place in which she would stand waving a handker-chief to relatives who were leaving after a summer visit.

All adult males with any connection to the deceased in life are expected to attend the funeral. Employers have to accept that during the year there will be many days when employees are absent because of funeral obli-gations. The first to carry the coffin are the closest friends and relatives. The chief mourner, the closest male relative, is at the head of the coffin. As the body is carried away from the place of the living a procession is formed with a dual line of men following the coffin, each of whom is to have an opportunity to carry it. The carriers move from the back to the front as the coffin is carried away. Two fresh carriers come from the back and the front two stand aside, bareheaded, watching the procession go past. At this stage a further separation may occur as those less strongly involved, having fulfilled their ritual obligation to carry the coffin in a last social contact with the deceased, may return to their usual activities. They do this as soon as they have watched the coffin pass by where they stand. Others carry on with the coffin to attend the actual burial. If the cemetery is far from the village they will be transported in hired buses. 'They may smoke while they are waiting. There is usually a lot of chat unless the funeral has hit them hard. There is no ceremony at the grave. By then there may not be many people left.'

The return from mourning behaviour appears abrupt. One observer commented that the actual burial 'seems to be just a job to be done'. There is no meal provided except for the closest relatives and those who have travelled far. People who are not closely involved rapidly return to the social processes of living. Shops reopen, washing is hung out and discussion of the deceased and the manner of death drops from the conversation.

This account of some observations of everyday activities in the Western Isles has been largely anecdotal. The intention has been to provide an impression of some of the aspects of kinship, village membership and home life which are the more important components of the cultural specificity of the islands. It is these aspects which set the area apart as a Community from the nation State of which it is a political and economic part and with which it shares some common cultural components. Yet it should be apparent in this account that the segregation of the Western Isles from the rest of the United Kingdom is a matter of degree. The individual Hebridean belongs to different groups for different purposes. Differing situations activate appropriate loyalties; to kin, to a village, to an island, to Scotland or to Britain.

The individual lives within the confines of a continuum of interlinked and overlapping behaviour patterns. These should not be conceptualised as concentric circles with the individual at the centre point and the layers reaching out from family to village to island to nation. The person is always decentred with respect to any such set of sociological circles. He does not move from the family circle if he travels to Inverness. His behaviour may be different there for some purposes but he is always somebody's brother, someone else's husband, another person's father. His interaction with the agencies of the State, such as the Highlands and Islands Development Board, is influenced as much by these kinship roles as it is by his role as a native of Stornoway or as a Hebridean. Because of the individual's own life-cycle he is not only decentred with respect to these concentric circles but also displaced. The individual is not a fixed point but experiences a lifetime of growth and decay, a dynamic set of roles according to age and experience, all of which place him differently within each circle. It is these considerations which have led to this anecdotal account of the Hebridean way of life, an account which has attempted to present a set of experiences rather than a set of generalisations. Generalisations belong to kinship theory, not to the lived experience which is the Hebridean inheritance.

7   Three ways of speaking

In the social life of Lewis there is one major paradox which permeates all relationships. On the one hand there is the extremely powerful force of presbyterian Christianity, on the other the spectre of alcoholism. To make a link between the two is no mere sociological exercise. The Churches, by their opposition to drinking, construct one kind of relationship. But more important is the implicit conceptual connection between two opposing behaviour patterns.

Up to this point there has been no delineation of what has been referred to as 'full Church membership'. The role of minister in presbyterian Churches has been described, but that of the Church member has been left unclear. This is partly because of the separation of protestant and Roman Catholic areas in the Western Isles. The account which follows deals only with the northern, protestant areas, principally Lewis. It attempts an explanation of one type of behaviour in a specific region. Yet it must be remembered that alcoholism is a general Scottish problem. Moreover, the difficulties experienced in Lewis are felt in some form in the southern islands of the Outer Hebrides. Compton Mackenzie immortalised the inhabitants of the southern isles in *Whisky Galore.* In that novel he fictionalised an actual incident in which a boat bearing a cargo of whisky was wrecked off a Hebridean island. In the story told by Mackenzie, the inhabitants outwitted customs officials and appropriated the cargo for their own consumption. In the book and the film which followed, the drinking habits of the islands are portrayed as joyful and Bacchanalian. But, as Euripides showed, consorting with the Bacchae can arouse attendant destructive forces.

Even in *Whisky Galore* a link is made between religion and alcohol. On his first appearance in the book a priest, Father Macalister, complains that he cannot offer 'so much as a wee snifter' to a guest and finally pours a glass of altar wine (Mackenzie, 1969, p. 35). Later there is some discussion of Sabbath observance which is vital to the problem of whether the inhabitants of two neighbouring protestant or Roman Catholic islands relieve the wreck of its cargo (ibid, p. 124). Mackenzie illustrates one aspect of the tangled relationship between God and the whisky bottle in one incident in the novel. Two crofters sit watching the dawn rise over the wreck, drinking from one of two whisky bottles which they have just been given.

'Oh, well, who would have thought when we were walking to Mass this morning that we would be sitting here like this before two o'clock?' said Hugh. 'We'll just have a bite to eat and then we'll get the cart and drive along to Kiltod. I want to give my bottle to Father James.'

'Och, I want to give him my bottle,' Jockey protested.

'We've all had a dram out of yours. Och, one's enough for him just now,' Hugh decided firmly. '*A Dhia*, there's six hundred thousand bottles where this came from.'

'*Tha gu dearbh, Uisdean. Tha gu dearbh*,' Jockey agreed, in his voice a boundless content. '*Uisge beatha gu leòir, taing a Dhia*. We'll chust be saying three Hail Marys, Hugh.'

'Ay,' the other agreed, 'for favours received.'

The two crofters knelt down, and mingling with the murmur of their prayers was the lapping of the tide along the green banks of Bàgh Mhic Ròin and a rock pipit's frail fluttering song. (ibid, p. 127).

The Gaelic words Mackenzie puts in the crofter's mouth, 'Yes indeed, Hugh. Yes indeed. Whisky galore, thanks be to God,' have the same repetitive ring as the 'Hail Marys' which he says with his friend. But this fictional linguistic link is more complex in the island reality and further complicated when it is mixed with the tenets of protestantism.

In Lewis the three principal Churches are the Free Church of Scotland, the Established Church of Scotland and the Free Presbyterian Church. The first has numerical precedence, yet in some ways it is the austere Calvinism of the last which has the strongest ideological influence. The Free Presbyterian Church had its source in the Scottish Reformation and the Covenanters. It is possibly the closest to Knox's ideal of Christianity, espousing a doctrine of self-denial and other-world orientation in which the most influential notion is the idea of the Elect. The Elect are those chosen by God for salvation. The choice can only be made by the Almighty, good works alone do not qualify the individual for redemption. This means that the Churches in a strictly protestant area such as Lewis effect a separation of the population; less between religious and non-religious than between those who are chosen by God and those who can only wait to be chosen. Thus the socio-religious life of this area is dominated by the notion of the conversion or *curam*. This conversion is close to the model of Saul on the Road to Damascus in which the omnipotent power of God alters even the most unwilling individual.

The members of the Churches, particularly the Free Church and Free Presbyterian Church, are distinguished from the rest of the congregation in both dress and action. Only members take communion and their right to do this is established through showing the Marks of Jesus. One minister described the qualities of members whom he called 'Christians in the strict sense'. They are 'God-centred. Their religion is not just a matter of opinion. The making of a Christian is a work of the Holy Spirit, which is irreversible. We try to keep this distinction very clear.' An individual becomes a true Christian 'through being born again, by having the marks of being born again which distinguishes it from superficial religion. These are the desire to please Jesus in everything he does and seeking holiness in everything he does.'

Thus members, who take communion, are distinguished from adherents, who contribute to parish funds and whose names are on the parish register. Communicant members of the Free Church and Free Presbyterian Church are a people apart: the 'clique of the converted' as one anthropologist has phrased it (Parman, 1972, p. 169).

A few cynical non-converted persons describe the clique as a 'social club' whose members sit together in Church, shake hands with each other more often than with non-members, and are always having meetings in each others' houses from which others are excluded . . . the non-converted often express envy, and say that they wish they felt the same way that the converted people seem to feel (ibid, p. 170).

The exclusiveness of people who have been converted or 'had the *curam*' is due partly to their obvious withdrawal to the sacred sphere. Their dress, behaviour, life pattern and conversation are all likely to be noticeably different from the rest of the population.

There are tales of sudden conversions. The story of the habitual drunkard who was spending his evening as usual in a 'bothan' or drinking club, is typical. Suddenly his face was seen to change and he put down his drink. He left the 'bothan' and was never seen there again for he straightway joined the Church and became a true Christian. The half-empty glass is reputed to remain on the shelf where he had left it, a memorial to his conversion. Such narratives may have a grain of truth, they illustrate the feeling that God's choice must be recognisable and must change the individual. A sudden conversion is thus the ideal and a violent change of life-style from profligacy to asceticism is conceptually preferable. But few conversions take this form. It is more usual for the individual to begin to think about Jesus, to dream of the Bible or to have the words of the psalms and hymns running constantly in the mind. Once a person feels that he or she has been chosen by God, sober behaviour and dress are required. The acolyte begins to join the company of those who are already converted, whose conversation turns often to Jesus and who go not only to the regular Sunday services but also to weekday prayer meetings.

The crux of the *curam* is the communion. In order to partake of the sacrament of wafer and wine the individual must be accepted as a member by the Church Session. This is the point at which secular and sacred spheres articulate. It is at the time of communion that the members are symbolically differentiated from the rest of the congregation. But it is also at the communion that secular life and sacred life intersect.

Communions in each village take place twice a year, in spring and autumn. The same weekend is used by all presbyterian denominations in the village. Thus the communions are village events which affect the lives of all inhabitants to some extent. But they are not events which are exclusive to the village for they are the occasion of much inter-village and even inter-island visiting. These religious observances operate to include all village members but they also provide opportunities for relationships which have a basis in religion and override village and kinship links. The village congregations are obliged to offer hospitality to members of other congregations, who visit for the weekend in order to take part in the communion services. This is symbolised in the fact that the officiating ministers are also visitors from other areas. In one village many women complained to me about the exhaustion and expense involved in providing hospitality for known and unknown visitors who might also stay overnight.

The entire communion weekend is regarded as a holy time. Schools close on Thursday and shops often cease trading for some or all of the time. There are two gatherings a day from Thursday to Monday and the already large local congregations are swelled by visitors from other areas.

The pattern of religious activity during these five days emphasises the distinction between sacred and secular spheres. Thursday is the day of atonement and confession, when the emphasis is on sin and the remembrance of sin. In a sense this confirms the common sinful origins of all humanity and thus includes the entire congregation. Friday was traditionally the day of the Men. It verbally separates the Christian and non-Christian. This is the day of affirmation when laymen publicly confess what it is that makes them Christian and the day of questioning when those who wish to take communion are examined by the Church session for the Marks of Christ.

Saturday is the day of preparation for the communion service on Sunday. During communion the congregation itself is segregated into Christian and non-Christian. The central pews reserved for communicants are marked by white cloths. In the communion sermon there is usually reference to the fellowship of communicants, so that the separation is both spatially and verbally marked as well as ritually observed.

Sunday evening and Monday services are for thanksgiving, the sermons emphasising that salvation is obtained through Grace alone. There is frequent reference to those who are not saved, who have perhaps committed the unforgivable sin of denying the Holy Ghost and are thus condemned to eternal death. Prayers and sermons alike abound with verbal symbolism and use of contrast, sin versus salvation, life versus death and men versus God. The only possible mediation is God's Grace which chooses those who are to be saved from sin for eternal life.

Running through all religious life on the island is a constant awareness of the word of God. The Biblical text, as explained in Chapter 5, is used as a source of infallible reference and many of the religious community have a detailed knowledge of chapter and verse. One result of this is that Biblical quotation is frequently used to enforce arguments or settle disputes. It is not unusual for local newspaper notices of thanks for help during illness or bereavement to end with a Bible reference. A typical example would be Psalm 48.14: 'For this God is our God for ever and ever: he will be our guide even unto death.'

The presbyterian influence on the island is publicly opposed to the use of alcohol and this has had very important social consequences. But one should be wary of positing a direct cause and effect connection between puritanical opposition and the incidence of alcoholism. The Churches may well be espousing and reinforcing feelings of fear and revulsion against what is experienced as a pressing social problem. Religious leaders have been influential in restricting the public use of alcohol to weekday consumption in hotels mainly situated in Stornoway. There was a short time when prohibition ruled in Lewis. Yet it is often said that in the referendum, which led to alcohol being banned from the island under a Scottish law, it was the female vote as much as the Church vote which won the day. It is the women's fear of abuse of alcohol rather than male use of alcohol as a masculine assertion which is most noticeable to a female researcher. Throughout Lewis and Harris one question above all was put to me by the women with whom I spoke. 'Does your husband take a drink?', was the query, meaning specifically 'Does he drink whisky?' And there would be a nod of agreement or sigh of relief when I said that he did not.

The extent of the problem of alcoholism is difficult to assess. Statistical evidence would seem to indicate that the incidence of alcoholism on Lewis is one of the highest in the United Kingdom. The recognition of any social problem usually occurs through the use of some officially accredited form of statistics. These can be useful in assessing official attitudes to what is or is not a 'problem' and as a guide to the size and scope of the problem once it is so designated. But official statistics are not the true measure of the problem of alcoholism in the Hebrides and in any case there is no coherent State policy from which a statistical appraisal can be drawn. What is important is the Hebridean assessment of the use and abuse of alcohol on the islands, the local recognition of a local problem. All islanders are aware of its existence. As if imparting secret information most informants would confidentially report, 'We have a drink problem here you know'.

Yet this confidential knowledge is not allowed to intrude in the literature on the islands without fierce opposition from the Hebrideans themselves. In 1949 Alisdair Alpin MacGregor published a book, *The Western Isles*, which included a savage attack on the islanders' morals and values, particularly their drinking habits. Moreover he suggested that the Hebrideans were idle and an unnecessary burden on the British taxpayer (MacGregor, 1949). MacGregor's own approach to the islands is interesting. He is surely the author fictionalised by Compton Mackenzie as 'Hector Hamish Mackay'. Mackenzie includes in *Whisky Galore* some passages, supposedly taken from H.H. Mackay's books, containing lyrical sentences such as 'We stand entranced midway along Tràigh Swish and watch the placid ocean break gently upon the sand to dabble it with tender kisses' (Mackenzie, 1969, p. 167). Such purple-prose romanticism is not too far removed from MacGregor's style in his early, glowing accounts of the remote and misty islands from which he claimed ancestry (MacGregor, 1933). *The Western Isles* shows an extreme change in attitude, from Hebridean idyll to Hebridean nightmare; evidence of painful and personal disillusion.

The island response to the new book was swift. During the 1940s and 1950s a local body, the Lewis Association, was engaged in producing factual reports on the island which, it was hoped, would influence State policy. The Lewis Association devoted Report Number 6 to 'countering the attack on the good name of the people of the Hebrides' (Lewis Association, No. 6, p. 5).

MacGregor is attacked for being 'a person of pronounced views. He is an anti-vivisectionist, he is a vegetarian and a total abstainer. These are sound properties in a propagandist or a reformer, but they are not the best qualifications for a person who poses as an unbiased observer, or seeks to give a balanced picture of conditions as they really are' (ibid, p. 9). The Report then gives a 'Critical Analysis of the Book' in which it accuses MacGregor of 'errors of fact' which are often nothing to do with the drink problem. The book, according to the Report, 'from beginning to end is riddled with similar contradictions, inconsistencies, illogicalities, distortions and blunders in large matters as in small' (ibid, p. 12). When the Report turns to giving a 'True Picture' of Lewis people it states that 'they are peasants; they are descended from warriors and sea-rovers; they are separated from the ways of living of cities by mountains and wastes of seas' (ibid, p. 34). A drink problem is admitted but it is suggested that it is exaggerated and on the wane.

Fanatical opposition to alcohol consumption is thus joined to a similar opposition to the idea of an alcoholism problem. But any exaggeration of the abuse of drink on the islands is no less misleading than the romantic exaggerations of writers like MacGregor in his early work. The choice is not between a picture of the islands as misty and idyllic or as blurred by over-indulgence in drink, since it is possible to view the social situation of the islanders without resorting to either romantic haze or savage criticism.

The exchange between Alisdair Alpin MacGregor and the Lewis Association took place in the 1950s. But similar disagreements occur regularly. In 1978 a local newspaper reported on the apparent existence of a drink problem among employees of *Comhairle nan Eilean* and its obvious concern that people with such difficulties should obtain help without losing their employment. Yet bitter denials of the existence of any such problem appeared in the newspaper during the following week. Just as the researcher is told of alcoholism in confidence, so the problem cannot be given public recognition. It is through this refusal to assimilate the extent of the problem that alcoholism becomes an obstacle and an enigma.

The most distressing aspect of the Lewis drink problem for an outsider is the lack of public disapproval of its daily occurrence. But to state that is to present a subjective evaluation and comparison and can give the erroneous impression that the streets of Stornoway are perpetually thronged with drunks. This is not the case. But the incidents of drunken behaviour do have some characteristic qualities. The most striking feature is that obvious occurrence of drunkenness is usually ignored. This might not seem to differ from the reaction of the public towards alcoholics in urban situations. Most cities have their known alcoholics who frequently take up regular street positions and perform a known set of antics. Unless their behaviour becomes obscene, violent or too bizarre the public tend to ignore them and the police do not take them into custody. But they are treated as external to social concerns by all but charitable institutions or occasionally the State-organised social services. They have no role other than as 'alcoholic'; they are outside society.

Of course these individuals conform to the popular conception of the alcoholic as a social outcast, related to other inadequates such as drug users and the permanently homeless. But the more common face of alcoholism is the gradual extension of social drinking into a compulsion which destroys social behaviour, family and employment. This is a pressing problem in Western society but one which is usually hidden from public view.

In Lewis the public and private faces of the drink problem merge. Individuals who have clearly over-indulged in alcohol and exhibit bizarre and unsocial behaviour are nevertheless greeted publicly with no apparent censure, even though the opinion that 'he has a drink problem' or 'he was awa in the heid' may later be expressed. A man who is obviously the worse for drink is not shunned, nor is it common to see an attempt made to remove him from a public situation in order to return him to sobriety. Instead it is much more usual for people to act as if nothing is out of place, to ignore the social incapacity of the drunk and act as if the situation were 'normal'. This may be partly the result of living in the type of social situation in which criticism cannot be publicly voiced. Plate 15 records one incident which illustrates the apparent equanimity with which drunkenness is treated. The man in the picture was staggering along the main street of Stornoway one Friday lunchtime. He was alone and obviously incapable of sensible action. With arms raised he stumbled into the path of several cars effectively bringing the traffic to a halt and mouthing some unintelligible speech to the horizon. An agent of law and order was present in the shape of a traffic warden. He stepped goodnaturedly into the road and gently moved the drunken man towards the pavement where he continued to lurch on an unsteady course towards the harbour, virtually unremarked by passers-by.

The lack of recognition of alcoholism is accompanied by an inability to recognise the incidence of depressive illness. Statistical evidence shows that Lewis has a high rate of clinically diagnosed depressive illnesses although the incidence of those mental states defined as schizophrenic is somewhat lower than in the rest of the United Kingdom. There has been little research on this issue but the two problems seem to be linked in a generalised Hebridean self-image which is well captured in the last lines of the poem about Eskimos, 'Some pathetic relic of a butchered past.' It is only rarely that this feeling is given more than rhetorical form. But on one occasion an informant referred to the picture of decline and decay drawn in

103

Plate 15. Friday lunchtime incident in Stornoway.

Inishkillane, a book which has been quite widely read on the island. This Lewisman commented: 'It's a painful book for us to read up here. We almost want to reject it, for it is our experience which is described.'

This particular islander referred specifically to the mental illness of 'Joseph Murphy' which Brody uses as a key issue in his description of de-moralisation. Joseph Murphy is an elderly bachelor suffering from a progressive sense of social isolation. Loneliness and lack of an acceptable social role leads to successive, pathetic, mental breakdowns, one of which is graphically described in the book. Brody's contention is that the demoralisation of individuals like Joseph Murphy is a social phenomenon, 'they feel outside their social system, and they have no faith in its continuing' (Brody, 1974, p. 16). Thus, according to Brody, the individual's social isolation is a concomitant of the community's sense of isolation. 'Inishkillane began to feel itself to be a peripheral part of a single culture' (ibid, p. 99). It is this same sense of periphery which dominates the Hebridean self-image. It is not just a feeling of being on the edge but the insecurity which arises from the sensation that one might fall or be pushed off. Referring to Joseph Murphy, my informant said: 'I know him. I've seen that. He could be my cousin or my uncle.'

The conception of periphery or of being in some way the last bastion arises constantly in the speech of Hebrideans. On one occasion I reluctantly recorded the following words at the virtual dictation of the Melbost bard. 'How I envy people who haven't got the same problem of the Gaels of fighting with our backs to the wall to keep our language and culture from being swamped and overwhelmed. Here we are, the remnants of the Celtic race, gradually chased to the West and struggling to keep something.' My reluctance related to the circumstances in which these words were recorded. These reflections on the cultural homogeneity of the Hebrides are part of a much longer text. I was ostensibly recording information regarding the rituals surrounding birth, marriage and death, but the bard constantly broke off his replies to my questions to insert passages regretting two elements which for him seemed to have damaged his Gaelic heritage. The first was the 'rationalism' of Calvinist doctrine. The old faith, he claimed, 'has much more than the puritanical faith' which 'came up from the south.' Rationalism with its demand for proof destroyed the 'mysticism of the old religion with which you could ornament your writing'. The second element he mentioned, also originating from the south, is 'sophistication' which he considered had entered island life by the 1930s. 'We are not immune' he said, 'to the sophisticated society that surrounds us. With the shrinking of the world and man conquering space our remoteness has disappeared. Nothing is immune.'

At the time of recording this text I was vaguely annoyed that the bard's insistent comments on the fall of Gaeldom interrupted the flow of information on life-cycle rituals. But this testimony should be examined not just for the factors which an anthropologist finds interesting but also for the words with which in his anxious repetitions the bard kept uppermost those elements which most interested *him*.

While the bard claims that the Gaels on Lewis are fighting to preserve the remnants of a cultural tradition from puritanism and sophistication the observer on the island is soon aware of the importance of puritanism. Critics of 'traditionalism' in Lewis tend to blame not the Gaelic heritage but the power of the Churches to block the road to modernity. The Churches themselves take on this role by seeing the islands as the last bastion of Christianity in a misguided, agnostic or heretical world. The strength of this conviction reverberates in Free Church pronouncements. One annual Report on Religion and Morals contends:

The year . . . has passed leaving the flotsam of Britain's greatness as wreckage on the shore of time. Politically we are governed by the Left of the Labour Party, who now in communistic and atheistic zeal work the puppet who was our Wilsonian Institute. Economically we see no sure horizon, morally, we are trying to dig through bedrock, and in spiritual religious matters we have evicted God.

The style of the Report shows a typical Free Church use of language in which Biblical imagery is wrought with verbal symbolism. Sermons likewise use this style of oratory espousing a reiteration of religious cliché which gradually mounts into an anticipation of Doomsday and Judgement. Thus the Report ends:

We fear that the enemy of souls has, to a great extent undermined our foundations, but God sits on his throne. We still have true believers in Christ Jesus . . . and as we see the climax of the world inexorably approaching, we believe they will still be there when the cry rings out, 'Behold the Bridegroom cometh'. (Free Church, 1961).

The Free Church thus holds to the tenet that the majority of wise virgins are to be found in the Hebrides. The millennial tone is in keeping with the relatively short history of this Church. It is barely 135 years old. Yet it presents to the external world an image of Hebridean solidarity and regulates the cultural life of Lewis.

A recent meeting of the Lewis Schools Council decided that too many dances were being held at the main secondary school in Stornoway. It was agreed to write to *Comhairle nan Eilean* asking the Council to limit the number of dances organised. Dancing is disapproved of by the presbyterian faithful for it is believed to lead to licentiousness and drunkenness. In many places Church influences have prevented the use of village halls for dancing, and even in the past discouraged the erection of halls which might be used for village gatherings. Youth clubs have only really arisen on the island since 1968. The Churches disagreed with mixing the sexes after dark and had no established tradition of music and drama. But young people established clubs in village halls and, although Church influences spoke out against dances, there were no established village mechanisms which could regulate the use of halls for late-night Friday dances.

The separation of secular and spiritual spheres here operated to prevent the Churches' effective intervention. On the question of Sabbath observance the Church forms an efficient pressure-group but in such matters as dances concentration on the spiritual entails the individual's refusal to be involved in secular affairs. Thus one youth worker on the island commented that Church-oriented parents tend not to be particularly concerned about their children's nocturnal activities.

Examination of obituaries in the *Stornoway Gazette* reveals this strong emphasis on the importance of spiritual life. The religious progress of the deceased is often more of a concern than their secular lives. As one Lewisman commented, 'it is in obituaries that people reveal their ideal types'. In the same issue of the *Gazette* which reported the complaints about dances, a deceased native of Tong is described thus: 'Her upright character, her very regular attendance at church, and her exceptional knowledge of Scripture, led many discerning people to conclude that here was one touched by God's amazing grace' (*Stornoway Gazette*, 4 February 1978).

Further in the same issue, however, a contradiction occurs. The sobriety and grace referred to in the Church ideal contrast with the ideal expressed in other obituaries. The attribute of Grace is God-given and thus external to the essentially sinful individual. God chooses the elect, who are thus removed from the natural profane world to the spiritual sphere. Yet two other obituaries refer to men who were part of the company of 'nature's gentlemen'. The concept of nature's gentlemen is a direct contrast to the notion of original sin. In the one idea it is possible for the individual to possess grace as a natural attribute, in the other the individual can only be

saved from sin for Grace by the nod of Divine assent. That the two con-
ceptions coexist on Lewis is witness to the bard's distinction between the
old mysticism and the new puritanism.

Further examination of obituaries reveals that those referred to as
nature's gentlemen are usually granted the attribute of wit. Wit here means
both native intelligence and the ability to invent jokes, particularly verbal
witticisms in Gaelic. It is to this that the bard implicitly refers when he
speaks of the Gaelic mysticism with which one used to be able to 'ornament one's writing'. Wit is a creative attribute essentially manifested in
language. Significantly the only cultural component which has survived the
puritan invasion intact is the Gaelic language which is used as a symbol
both of the ancient tradition of Gaeldom and of the new puritan faith,
despite direct government intervention to suppress it.

It is possibly important to distinguish three major forms of Gaelic. The
formal archaic Gaelic of the Churches has a specific sung form of psalmody.
Broadcast Gaelic provides a form of received pronunciation. But there is a
wide variety of Gaelic dialects spoken in home and village life in rural areas.
In all three forms Gaelic is a living language, but the style and context vary.

In its everyday form, Gaelic exists largely as an oral medium. The users
tend to be bilingual speakers of Gaelic and English, but are more likely to
be fully literate only in the latter language. Many Gaelic-speakers lack a
full range of vocabulary in this tongue, as their use of it is limited to
specific contexts. Gaelic is not the language of bureaucracy, the law or
technology. Until recently it has not been the language of education or of
literacy.

Paradoxically the early history of Gaelic reveals it to have been a literate medium of some social importance. An early historical distinction can
be made between classical literary form and vernacular Scottish Gaelic
(Thomson, 1974, p. 30). In the bardic tradition a heroic mode was adopted
and sentimental Gaelic songs seldom appeared until after the clan system
was destroyed and mixed cultural values were adopted (ibid, p. 88).
According to a Lewis-born Celtic scholar, Derrick Thomson, the commonest
theme of Gaelic poetry in the last century was nostalgia for a 'paradise
lost'. He attributes this partly to the uprooting caused by the Clearances.
But a further change was linguistic; the introduction of English led to a
debasement of written style (ibid, p. 223).

Evangelism affected not only the content but also the style of Gaelic.
The rhetorical mode of Lewis ministers in the 1970s reflects the concerns
and approach of early evangelism. Religion served a social purpose in providing a coherent set of values during the uncertainties of the Clearances.
But it also entered the linguistic territory of the Highlands and Islands,
providing a new formal mode for a language whose cohesion was under
threat of dissolution. The longest poem of Dugald Buchanan, poet and
evangelist, is entitled *The Day of Judgement*. It places great emphasis on
the pains of hell, with the damned featuring more prominently than the
righteous. Significantly, Buchanan was instrumental in the publication of

the first Gaelic translation of the Bible in 1767 (ibid, pp. 204–9). The poetry of the nineteenth century exhibits a strong religious element, which is more noticeable than any poetry of protest which arose from the exigencies of the Clearances. Criticism of landlords tended to be confined to the oral poetry of village bards. Once again a separation existed between speech and written form.

The twentieth century has produced what Thomson calls the poetry of innovation. The sophistication complained of by the bard has been introduced alongside the universal penetration of English, and it should perhaps be remembered that sophistication in its original sense is connected with debasement and adulteration. Thomson comments that 'There is now no linguistic hinterland to which the Gaelic writer can retire . . . the dice are heavily loaded against the survival of a secure Gaelic personality' (ibid, p. 250). Moreover, a further division exists between the village Gaelic and the non-traditional Gaelic of academics and professionals. According to Thomson this new Gaelic is not only bilingual but also bicultural. Many modern Gaelic writers import elements of English or 'Western' culture into their published work. Thus one Lewis-born poet, Iain Crichton-Smith, who now has a national reputation, has been known to utilise psychoanalytic metaphor in his verse:

and I do not know your road at all
you in the half-light of your sleep
haunting the bottom of the sea without rest,
and I hauling and hauling on the sea's surface
(from: 'You are at the Bottom of my Mind', ibid, p. 276).

It has been claimed that this self-conscious reformulation of Gaelic is the inevitable result of emigration of bilinguals from their home area. Where Gaelic is the language of hearth and home, part of the bilingual's linguistic repertoire, it operates merely as a given. But when the bilingual individual leaves the home context he becomes aware of the components of a language which is strange to monoglots in the external world. Thus it is not surprising that much of the impetus to check the decline of Gaelic comes from those who are now outside the Gaelic community (Macleod, 1969, pp. 86–7).

Alongside the cultural given of Gaelic rests the puritan inheritance of the nineteenth century, which is also now a given component of Lewis life. Acceptance of the obligations of presbyterian faith is often taken for granted in the pattern of family life. The Biblical text, accepted in its infallible entirety, becomes an accepted feature of the social and psychological environment. This is possibly reinforced because the skills of reading are often taught and practised using the Biblical text. Traditional Gaelic mysticism continues in the Biblical mode, 'now the voice they heard was the voice of God, speaking to them directly, and using the words of the Biblical texts they had memorised previously' (ibid, p. 92). The uneasy fusion of the two cultural components has had a direct effect upon the oral tradition of Gaeldom, 'The island tradition could not withstand the introduction of a *written* version of other people's lore: and now the artistic work in which they delight and from which they repeatedly sing and quote, is the Bible' (ibid, p. 227).

The previous mysticism which contained a store of now largely forgotten folk-tales and legends may have been supplanted by the myths of the Judeo-Christian faith. But Lewis people do maintain an oral tradition which is primarily historical in its orientation and reflects the theme of 'paradise lost'. This lost paradise is the realm of nature's gentlemen, situated before the Clearances as far back as folk-memory can be traced. 'When my people were evicted' is one common theme. Eviction, emigration and natural disaster are the three major components. This is also reflected in the Gaelic media. Not only do the islanders tell these tales to each other and the interested visitor, they also write or record them so that they can be re-read or re-broadcast back to the islands. One common reiteration is the voyage of the *Metagama*. This ship was one of the liners which carried large numbers of Lewis emigrants to the Americas during the 1920s. Another favourite story tells of the *Iolaire* disaster, when the boat returning survivors of the First World War to the island sank in Stornoway harbour on New Year's Day, 1919. The bodies were washed up on the beaches alongside presents which the returning soldiers and sailors were bringing for their families. The collective grief of islanders, who had already suffered disproportionate losses during the war, lingered long past the generation which was directly affected.

Alongside these oral traditions are written histories of 'paradise lost' and the manner of losing it. Lewis people often tacitly refuse to discuss their own experience of 'history', preferring to present instead a copy of the 'real history' of Lewis. This was written by a Lewisman, W.C. Mackenzie. Its profits were dedicated to a fund for a memorial to those lost in the Great War and the *Iolaire* disaster (Mackenzie, 1919). But this book deals less with history than pre-history, with speculation, comparison, etymology and archaeology. The times to which Mackenzie refers are mythical rather than chronological. What he is concerned to establish above all is the viability of descriptions like 'peasant', 'warrior' and 'sea-rover', the categories utilised by the Lewis Association.

Mackenzie is not always meticulous in citing his references. Much of his narration seems to have been taken from the Morrison Manuscripts, which in his day were unpublished. This is a set of stories of the clans on Lewis which was put together from oral testimony by a Stornoway cooper in the early nineteenth century. Morrison appears to have made his handwritten collection purely for his own satisfaction. But he represents a Lewis tradition. In the present century Dr Macdonald of Gisla also collected a set of written and already published accounts of local history which were printed as *Tales and Traditions of the Lews*. This is another source of 'authentic history' to which the researcher is often directed. The collection is not unified by any principle other than 'Lewis'. The subjects covered are familiar recent history such as the Deer Raids in Park (see p. 24). Macdonald's concern to record what is already known and thus render it more tangible is not unique on the island. In Stornoway Town Library on most days one can see elderly men who occupy themselves by ferreting indiscriminately through already published accounts in newspapers. They add piles of notes to those they have previously collected together with photographs and occasional photocopies at home in some cardboard box. These are the men to whom the researcher is referred as 'being able to tell you all about the island'. It is always assumed that researchers wish to know about the past. Few interviewees fail to mention historical events, many refer to Pictish and Celtic pre-history. But the stories I was told were always the same stories I had read before commencing fieldwork. The constant repetition can thus be viewed as a mythic narration of symbolic significance.

The Hebridean self-image is built on a myth of past coherence. The over-whelming necessity is to construct a lost paradise which can be contrasted with present contradiction. As has been shown in previous chapters the traditional Hebridean or crofting way of life can be argued to be an academic construction. It cannot be contrasted with a sociological construct like modernity. But this should not mask the importance of the construction of tradition by the islanders themselves. Such a myth performs a vital social function. Paradise can be regained as well as lost and for the people of Lewis it provides a single thread of coherence against the contrasting sets of norms which their present existence presents. The people of Lewis are not experiencing social problems because of the intrusion of modernity into a synchronic traditional way of life. The situation is more complex. There is not merely a contrast or conflict between Gaelic and English cultures as Thomson suggests. On the contrary the conflict of values is, as the bard indicated, tri-cultural. The contradictory norms of three value systems, Gaelic, Puritan and English, produce a situation similar to that somewhat unclearly designated 'anomie' by Brody in *Inishkillane*. Thus it is significant that one informant should have spoken to me of the breakdown of Joseph Murphy. It was a rare statement of recognition.

8 The future returns to the past

Preceding chapters have attempted to examine the idea that the Hebridean 'Community' is not a vestigial part of the United Kingdom. It has been shown that the development of the specific cultural characteristics of the Western Isles have a history which has been produced through the development of capitalism in Britain. The changing culture of the islands is not the result of modern or industrial structures invading a static traditional form. Yet it has also been shown that the idea of a static and coherent past is used to justify both State policy and Hebridean activity.

Most descriptions of the Hebrides return to the past. This book has been no exception. But the intention here was to re-examine the received wisdom of standard historical and sociological accounts. In the media a different approach is taken. The idea of the traditional peasant culture of the Hebrides is a stereotype in British culture. Unfortunately it penetrates both the Hebridean consciousness and State agencies.

In 1973 it became clear that the North Sea Oil Boom had reached the Hebrides. Local newspapers began printing headlines like STORNOWAY GETS THE SHEIKS. The Stornoway Trust was approached by the British-based subsidiary of a Norwegian shipping company, which negotiated for a lease on land which they intended to use for oil-related industrial production. As explained in Chapter 4 the hopes raised by this company were short-lived but at the time much concern was expressed about the effect which large-scale industrial production would have upon the crofting way of life. The problem was approached as if industrial production and wage labour were both new to the Hebrides.

Once the difficulties about Sunday working had been settled it appeared as if the crofting way of life could be preserved, such is the strength of the idea that the Church on Lewis represents the traditional form of social life. Several additional strategies were employed by State agencies in order to buttress the power of the Church. Throughout the Highlands and Islands the sudden appearance of oil-related industry had presented acute problems to local councils. In several places the population had risen beyond local capacity to deal with housing even on a temporary basis. The large oil-platform construction yards had not just had environmental effects upon the Highland landscape. They had been the cause of immense migrations of single men into small rural villages. Although the construction companies had provided work camps and even cruise liners to house their employees, the social problems for small communities had been enormous, and for some villages and islands the results permanently destroyed certain elements in everyday life.

If Olsen's had intended to import foreign labour into the Hebrides on such a scale then perhaps their development might have had wide-ranging effects upon the crofting way of life, however this is construed. But it was built into the terms of their lease that local labour should be used wherever possible, and the only major problem envisaged was the provision of adequate housing and other infrastructural services for return migrants. As the development was projected it would progress in five stages towards maximum output and the possible construction of oil-platforms. The difficulties could be staggered. It was estimated that over seven years 1,000 new houses would be needed. Even if Olsen's grew to full capacity in four years only 250 new houses a year would be needed. As the rate of building at that time was eighty houses a year it was thought that the island could cope with the lower figure. The only problem was that the local authority would need to acquire additional building land. In the Impact Survey prepared for the Stornoway Trust it was suggested that a housing plan should be made for the whole area on the basis of the Olsen development. It was felt that this plan should include rural as well as urban areas, for new housing might act as a stimulus to rural life if Lewis Offshore workers with young families moved into villages which had a predominantly ageing population.

The notion that new housing should be dispersed throughout the island stimulated one controversy which underlines the importance of the Hebridean myth for external observers. The issue revolved around the Callanish stones. This prehistoric circle of standing stones is similar in structure to Stonehenge. It stands alongside a village on the west side of Lewis. The Callanish stones were excavated, while Matheson was the landlord, from the thick peat which had hidden them for centuries. The excavation caused the removal of two croft houses. In 1974 a farm close to the stones was offered for sale. A local councillor regarded this site as ideal for housing development and his suggestion was taken up by the local authority. In the controversy which followed, the historical importance of the standing stones and their symbolic function as part of the Hebridean tradition grew somewhat out of proportion compared with the social and economic situation of the island.

Two articles in reputable national journals illustrate this, although less responsible reports appeared in national newspapers. A sociological article notable for many inaccurate statements about island life and history appeared in *New Society*. It began dramatically.

On a grassy knoll, at the end of a road linking scattered crofts in Callanish, a small settlement on the West Coast of the Hebridean island of Lewis, is a circle of jagged standing stones. Seen from a distance they could be the ruins of a crofter's barn. Close to, the stones are mystically rather than monumentally impressive, sticking up out of the saturated peat like petrified prehistoric vertebrae (Weightman, 1974, p. 741).

The proximity of the 'crofter's barn' and the 'prehistoric vertebrae' gives a clue to the tone of the article. The Hebrides are here being treated as artefacts not from history but from pre-history. The remoteness and strangeness implied in the Hebridean myth is underlined by the term 'mystically'. Later the writer states that the archaeologist Professor Thom has developed a theory about the standing stones concerning prehistoric astronomical alignments.

It is suggested that the proposed housing development would entail the destruction of the stones. This was never proven, but did give rise to many journalistic speculations. Despite local apathy, even hostility, towards the stones, certain archaeological interests were immediately mobilised in their defence. A Callanish Stones Society was formed. A second article appeared, this time in the *Architect's Journal*. The author states:

Nobody involved in this argument wants to see the islands becoming a frozen museum piece and without some kind of development continuing depopulation will advance their decay. But it is becoming increasingly clear that only a multi-disciplinary analysis of the island will produce a comprehensive plan and bring an understanding of Lewis's cultural origins during the third millenium BC (Webber, 1975, p. 709).

For the second millennium A.D. the same writer takes the most pessimistic housing figures as his criterion and ignores the fact that a seven-year build-up of the Olsen development is more likely.

There seems to be no conventional way of providing the 250 houses per annum since the island not only has no building contractor (the last went into liquidation in 1973) but a large percentage of existing sub-standard housing also needs urgent work. The freighting surcharge on materials to the islands is largely covered by grants, but outside contractors are obviously loath to tender for diffuse local authority housing in such isolated and climatically hostile conditions (ibid).

But within these pessimistic assertions there are several inaccuracies. In 1971, shortly before the oil industry reached Lewis, 910 people were employed in building and construction on the island. The majority were working for the three construction firms which have more than fifty employees. These enterprises may not be primarily Lewis-based but they are long established on the island. This is shown in the organisation of the construction industry labour force. It was in the construction industry that trade union activity first became effectively organised in Lewis. The firm which went into liquidation in 1973 continued to complete its contracts through the provision of support by the local authority.

Both articles reiterate the myths of backwardness and history. The article in *New Society* does contrast the needs of the archaeological community with those of the crofting community. But the crofting community is described as if it is a vestigial artefact. Thus the author writes of the peat 'so rich in relics and poor in houses' (Weightman, 1974, p. 743). When a Free Church minister says grace in the author's presence this is described as 'unnerving piety'. Moreover the writer also appears to have a typical misconception about the nature of oil-related development on Lewis. 'To hear the oily southern drawl of a Houston Texan among the Gaelic greetings of islanders at Stornoway airport is to feel a slight chill' (ibid). In most newspaper reports of the effects of North Sea Oil on the Highlands and Islands, the 'Oil Industry' is often treated as an animate subject with either a Ten Gallon Hat or an Arab burnous. The mythical 'Oil Industry' is then contrasted with the equally mythical 'traditional community'. This popular picture reflects the sociological cliché of tradition and modernity. But on Lewis the oil-related industry was Norwegian-based and the *New Society* article simply underlines the way in which stereotypes are employed. It also reveals a misunderstanding of one important aspect of island life, emigration. It is relatively common to hear Canadian or American accents among the lilting island voices as emigrant relatives come 'home' for holidays. The 'slight chill' felt by the author should not be for some supposed invasion but for the waves of emigration which have been one historical result in the Hebrides of the development of capitalism in the rest of the United Kingdom. Depopulation is hardly a new feature of island life. It has been a consistent element for two centuries: perhaps it might now be regarded as traditional.

The suggestion of housing development at Callanish did not become a concrete fact. It never really posed a serious threat to the standing stones. But the treatment of the suggestion in the media illustrates the way in which the islands are represented to the nation of which they are a part. Islanders did not rise to protect the stones in any number, but they became a national issue. When a large rise in local rates was caused by the withdrawal of the Rate Support Grant by central government the islanders showed themselves capable of spontaneous political action. A large public meeting was held and a well-organised Ratepayers' Association formed. This event was televised, but only for regional news. It was transmitted back to the islanders for whom rate rises were already a burning issue. National media did not pay attention to the results of the withdrawal of central government support. It is not newsworthy that the Western Isles lack certain public services which are common to most of the nation. The debate regarding the extent to which public services in some parts of a governmental unit such as Britain, can be allowed to fall below a minimum level did not reach the national press. The question of the potential use of the islands as a disposal area for nuclear waste greatly concerned the islanders in 1976 and 1977. This similarly barely received a mention in the national media. And the impact of the oil industry on the Western Isles was reduced to a national controversy over its effects on a stone circle, which 'has until recently remained obscure, compared with Stonehenge' (Weightman, 1974, p. 741).

This provides an example of the way a constructed view of the Hebrides affects media representation. Similar ideas about the Hebrides affect State policy, as was seen in Chapter 4. The Highlands and Islands Development

Board is caught in the contradiction of preserving the Crofting Way of Life by importing the growth-oriented policies appropriate to industrial areas. As has already been shown, the way of life experienced in the Western Isles is not a static ahistorical condition but a distinctive form which has been produced through the history of capitalist relations and State intervention on the islands.

One of the paradoxes which occurs in this situation is that the mythical form of tradition is important to the islanders. It is clear that it provides a theme of past coherence to counteract the insecurity aroused by changes which do not appear relevant to the area. The most interesting and hopeful aspects of Hebridean life in the 1970s are those which relate to this myth. There are efforts being made to strengthen the security provided by the myth, to give history credence and to develop a sense of community.

To a large extent the Western Isles remain as they were described in 1928, 'a remittance island' (Dougal, 1928, p. 54). Employment opportunities are scarce, particularly for young people. If the young want further education they have to leave the islands. The courses provided by the Lews Castle Technical College are principally for the acquisition of low-level engineering and catering skills. The college uses the mock gothic 'castle' built by Matheson in Stornoway which can be seen in the background of Plate 16. New buildings are being constructed as the courses increase in scope. Yet they still principally provide for the present limited range of island employment. Navigation courses aid the local fishing-industry, but also help young men to leave the island to join the merchant navy. Catering courses prepare young people for employment in mainland hotels. There is little outlet for engineering skills on the islands. Once the qualification is gained young people have the choice of leaving for the mainland or joining the large number of islanders who are receiving state remittances: 'on the Post Office' in the graphic local collective phrase.

So the pattern of permanent or temporary migration continues. In most cases it is an unwilling migration. Links with those members of the family who remain at home are maintained in most cases, often over several generations. One of the strongest elements of oral tradition is the reiteration of tales of migration. It is not uncommon for elderly people to recite the stories of journeys made across the Atlantic during the last century. Part of the myth of tradition is that the Hebridean way of life continues unchanged even in America, Canada and Australia. For those who have emigrated it is important to retain the ideal of the traditional way of life 'at home'. The idea of continuity is implicitly united with that of strength. This removes the anxiety that a secure Gaelic personality cannot remain intact. Thus Stornoway in Canada maintains a link with its mother town in Lewis. It is not unusual for letters from inhabitants of Gaelic-oriented areas which are geographically far removed from the Western Isles to be published in the *Stornoway Gazette*. Frequently the writer will stress the unbroken continuity of tradition in which Gaelic continues to be spoken and Free Church services are still held. When the *Gazette* appears at the

Plate 16. Lews Castle still dominates Stornoway, but it now houses a technical college.

end of the week there is a queue of people in the Stornoway post office sending the latest copy to absent relatives. Each summer brings a crop of tourists to the islands from Gaelic areas abroad. If they do not already have contacts in the islands their first stop is usually the library. The staff are adept at using local records to find the exiles some Hebridean cousins to visit.

Few of these tourists remain for more than a short time and most seem to be imbued with the myth of the misty islands. Those who do return to live in their island home are the temporary migrants who have been forced to spend their entire working life abroad and retire to croft or village life. This is one of the factors producing the imbalanced age-structure of the area. It has effects upon more than the social life of villages for it also influences the type and scope of State provision for the area. The maintenance of a Home Help Service for the elderly and handicapped takes up 59 per cent of the Social Services budget for the Western Isles.

Thus emigration is not the whole picture. Although the overall population figures indicate an outmigration both newcomers and returners settle in the islands. Newcomers often arrive for short periods only, often because of employment in some official position. Such individuals often bring their families and may settle in rural areas keeping sheep and cutting peats. The men become rapidly involved in island activities because of the nature of their employment. But they have a tendency to be critical of certain aspects of island life, particularly the Church in protestant areas. This criticism usually takes the form of a desire to improve or 'modernise' island habits and methods. It tends not to take account of the cultural specificity of the area. But this is a natural outcome of the type of employment which has brought these individuals to the islands. They are usually employees of a State agency which is committed to development. One notable feature of this group is the position of their wives who do not as a rule integrate well into female society on the island. They often suffer from restlessness, depression and a feeling of being trapped.

Two other groups of newcomers have chosen to live in the Hebrides. Both have been attracted by the romantic image. In the older generation is a small group of individuals who are interested in the history and culture of the islands and praise the 'way of life' without always being able to articulate what is good about it. They often marry locals and may bring up their children to be bilingual. The second is a younger group of people attempting to retreat from the 'pressures' of modern urban existence. They are noticeably different from other inhabitants in mode of dress and style of life. They praise the way of life and are able to articulate what they like about it: mostly those aspects which Hebrideans are rapidly discarding. Usually these newcomers are unable to adjust to life in the islands because they maintain an inflexible philosophy of what they regard as the good life. In most cases they leave disappointed after a relatively short stay. The locals blame the bad weather, hinting at their own native superiority in being able to withstand hardship. The strangers blame local lack of flexibility, and not infrequently use the letters column of the local paper to do so.

Few of these newcomers have any lasting effect upon local life. But by their questioning or reaffirmation of the Hebridean way of life they reinforce a tendency towards reflection or introspection. The category of returners tends to continue this process. Perhaps the most numerous returners are those referred to by one Lewisman as 'the dungaree brigade'. These are people who have had to leave to obtain employment or further education. They return at holiday time and make every attempt to take part in village life. To themselves, their relations and neighbours they give the impression of having 'roots' on the islands. People who retire to the islands are drawn from this group but many will never have the opportunity to return. Family disputes sometimes arise over which sibling will inherit the family croft and be able to return from the mainland.

This group contrasts with another smaller section of the inhabitants. The former type reaffirms the advantages of island existence. The latter calls these virtues into question by constantly raising to the level of a general issue their own inability to settle to island life. During fieldwork I labelled these individuals 'yoyos'. They moved perpetually between what they conceptualised as the island and the external world. In any model of brokerage they would provide the negative aspect, for they appeared to shift between opposing spheres without being able to integrate fully into either, and made regular crucial decisions to remain in one or the other.

These non-settlers contrast also with the returners who integrate at a young age into local life. Many are not, strictly speaking, returners. They are children of emigrants who marry Lewis spouses but already have strong family ties of their own in the Hebrides. Others are professionals whose sojourn on the mainland was always regarded as temporary. Many of those now employed as teachers, doctors and local officials left the islands simply to gain the qualifications necessary to return to a useful position in their home area. In both these cases there are few problems of adjustment and these individuals often take a leading part in town or village life.

But there is a new style of returner, of middle years, who would not previously have expected to return but who has been able to because of increased employment opportunities. These people tend to have married a spouse with Lewis connections but to have a young family born on the mainland. They have made a positive decision to return, which may have entailed a decrease in salary. The role they occupy is new and might be described as State-sponsored in that the employment opportunities are usually in the local authority or education spheres. Yet it should not be imagined that State policy has here provided the mainspring of modernisation. There have been many State policies directed towards the Hebrides, and few have been effective, at least in the sense that the effects achieved were those intended. What is important about these new policies is that they are locally regarded as appropriate and allow for development in a specifically Hebridean mode.

One of the most discussed aspects of State provision for the Western Isles is the Home Help Service. It gives employment to many women who would otherwise be unable to work and who are ineligible for either Social Security or Unemployment Benefit. As the age-structure of the area is so imbalanced there is obviously a necessity for some form of State aid. If the majority of people in a village is elderly it can strain community resources to the limit to provide sufficient care and attention for those who are unable to tend themselves.

Yet the Home Help Service is the object of constant criticism. Despite the clear indication of population figures many people feel that State aid in this field is unsuitable. It should not be necessary in the context of the Hebridean way of life. 'We need Lewis answers to Lewis problems' one local councillor stated. An elderly islander criticised the way in which he believed southerners send their parents into Old People's Homes at the first sign of infirmity: 'We look after our old people here. We love them.' Thus it is not surprising that this aspect of the Social Services should arouse the most anger. It is not congruent with the Hebridean self-image that the State should supplement family care in this way.

The problem for the Western Isles is therefore how to provide a continuity in the expressed mode of existence against increasing evidence that such a way of life is not viable. This does not imply that the Hebrides are attempting to counteract change or to maintain a static tradition. The main point about the specific culture of the Western Isles is not that it is static but that it has been remarkably flexible. During centuries of economic and political colonisation it has maintained a coherent sense of difference. It has achieved this despite increasing feelings of insecurity. The main weapon has not been entrenched tradition but the ability to adapt. As Gaelic has continued to be a living language despite a long history of change and repression, so the Hebridean integrity has continued. The ideal of the Crofting Way of Life has helped to maintain this by providing a myth of past coherence.

The strength of the social life in the Western Isles is thus not in tradition but in change. Yet such constant radical adaptation cannot be continued indefinitely and the ideal cannot survive in the face of social problems which deny its existence. The role of the new type of returner is to reconstruct the myths on a more secure basis. There are two aspects to the type of work involved. One has been the conscious discovery of community through the intervention of the Scottish Council for Social Services. The policy of this body is to encourage communities into voluntary action. In eight years of work on Lewis it has encouraged the emergence of Community Associations or Councils in every local area. This has provided a channel of communication between official bodies like the local authority and rural villages. It has also provided a means by which villagers can become involved in the provision of new or better local facilities such as clinics, recreation halls and even new biers. The success of the movement has been a noticeable feature of the 1970s throughout the islands as local committees are formed and people in rural areas become skilled in committee work. But it is difficult to judge whether this construction of community spirit will last despite the visible evidence of new halls and playing-fields throughout rural areas. What is clear is that the returners have a positive involvement in this sphere.

The major part of the reconstruction of Hebridean identity is concerned with language and history. Several projects aim to increase the use of Gaelic in contexts outside the home. Some are concerned to make education bilingual, to use Gaelic as a medium of instruction rather than as a subsidiary language like French or German. Thus when children learn history it is local history in the local language. Similarly there are local-history projects for adults, much recent Gaelic publishing, and a very new Gaelic theatre company, *Fir Chlis*. The conscious aim of the individuals involved in all these ventures is to return to the past in order to provide a secure base for the future. The aim is to give Hebrideans the opportunity to stand at the centre of their own history. If this is achieved the social problems of the area can be approached without the protecting veil of the old myth of 'tradition'.

Epilogue

Throughout this description of the changing cultures of the Western Isles the State has continued to be treated as if it were in some way external to the islands. But perhaps it could be argued that within the confines of this book it is not possible to account fully for the strategies employed by State agencies. These are themselves the result of a complex series of economic and political factors related on the one hand to industrial growth and on the other to the attendant politics of nationalism. Britain is best described as a multinational State. Within the boundaries of the major national entities several quite distinct cultural forms coexist. In the devolution debates of the 1970s it has been clear that the interests of these smaller entities are not being successfully served by the agents of central government. The Western Isles is one such entity. A realisation that its cultural specificity is not entirely due to the area being imprisoned in a previous historical state is the only chance it has to retain its distinct regional components. Without such a realisation there are two options. Either the islands will become progressively depopulated and lose social viability, or they will be assimilated into some bland version of 'British culture'.

If social anthropology has a role in the context of industrial nations it is to develop awareness of the different cultural forms which make up a nation State. Yet this does *not* entail a study of Communities in the sociological sense, for such entities are theoretically constructed and evaluated. They are not descriptions of 'reality'. The inhabitants of the Western Isles experience a lived existence which is the product of an historical process in which the development of the British State interacted with a specific Hebridean heritage. The task of the anthropologist is to try to understand this interaction as a dynamic process rather than to use the dichotomies of tradition and modernity, State and Community. These are ideological products of the historical process rather than explanatory tools with which to carry out social inquiry.

Bibliography

Arensberg, C. & Kimball, S. *Family and Community in Ireland*. Magnolia, Mass., 1940

Astbury, A.K. *The Black Fens*. Cambridge, 1958

Bell, C. & Newby, H. *Community Studies; an introduction to the sociology of the local community*. London, 1971

Blake, J.L. 'The Outer Hebrides Fisheries Training Scheme', *Scottish Studies*, Vol. 8, Part 1, 1964

Boissevain, J. 'Introduction' in Boissevain, J. & Friedl, J. (eds.) *Beyond the Community: social process in Europe*. The Hague, 1975

Brody, H. *Inishkillane: change and decline in the west of Ireland*. Harmondsworth, 1974

Buchannan, J.L. *Travels in the Western Hebrides from 1782 to 1790*. London, 1793

Calder, Rev. *After Seventy Years*. Stornoway, 1913

Chayanov, A.V. *The Theory of Peasant Economy*, Homewood, Ill., 1966

Collier, A. *The Crofting Problem*. Cambridge, 1953

Congested Districts Board. Reports of the Congested Districts Board for Scotland, 6th Report, 1904

Cottar Report. *Report to HM Secretary for Scotland on the Condition of the Cottar Population in the Lews*, 1888

Crofters' Commission, Annual Reports, 1966 & 1974

Crowley, D.W. 'The "Crofters' Party" 1885–1892', *Scottish Historical Review*, Vol. 35, No. 120, 1956

Davis, J. 'Beyond the Hyphen: some notes and documents on community–State relations in South Italy', in Boissevain & Friedl (eds.) (see under Boissevain, 1975, above)

Davis, J. *People of the Mediterranean: An Essay in Comparative Social Anthropology*. London, 1977

Dougal, H. 'Natural Resources of Lewis'. Dissertation for Diploma in Geography, University of Edinburgh, 1928

Emmett, I. *A North Wales Village*. London, 1964

Fenton, A. *The Island Black House*. London. 1978

Frankenberg, R. *Village on the Border: a social study of religion, politics and football in a North Wales community*. London, 1957

Franklin, S.H. *Rural Societies*. London, 1971

Free Church. 'Free Church Presbytery of Skye and Uist Religion and Morals Report.' Typescript, 1961

Gilbert, B. *British Social Policy, 1914–39*. London, 1970

Gillanders, F. 'The economic life of Gaelic Scotland today', in Thomson, D. & Grimble, I. *The Future of the Highlands*. London, 1968

Bibliography

Goodrich-Freer, A. *Outer Isles.* London, 1902
Grassic Gibbon, L. & MacDiarmid, H. *Scottish Scene, or the Intelligent Man's Guide to Albyn.* London, 1934
Gray, M. *The Highland Economy, 1750–1850.* Edinburgh, 1957
Gray, M. 'Crofting and fishing in the North-West Highlands, 1890–1914', *Northern Scotland,* Vol. 1, No. 1, 1972
Gregory, D. *History of the Western Highlands and Isles of Scotland from A.D. 1493 to A.D. 1625.* Edinburgh, 1836
The Guardian
Hardy, M. 'Report to the Rt. Hon. Lord Leverhulme: a survey of the Agricultural and Mineral Possibilities of Lewis and Harris.' Unpublished manuscript, Stornoway Public Library, 1919
Harris Tweed Association. *Harris Tweed Handbook.* (unpaginated), Stornoway, 1975a
Harris Tweed Association. *The Harris Times.* Stornoway, New York, 1975b
Harrison, M. 'The Peasant Mode of Production in the work of A.V. Chayanov', *The Journal of Peasant Studies,* Vol. 4, No. 4, 1977
Headrick, J. 'Report on the Island of Lewis' contained in a letter to the Rt. Hon. Lord Seaforth, the proprietor, 1800
Highland News (Western Edition)
Hodgson, W.C. *The Herring and its Fishery.* London, 1957
Hunter, J. 'The Politics of Highland Land Reform, 1873–1895', *Scottish Historical Review,* Vol. 53, 1974a
Hunter, J. 'The Emergence of the Crofting Community', *Scottish Studies,* Vol. 18, 1974b
Hunter, J. 'The Gaelic Connection: The Highlands, Ireland and nationalism, 1873–1922', *Scottish Historical Review,* Vol. 54, 1975
Hunter, J. *The Making of the Crofting Community.* Edinburgh, 1976
Johnson, S. *A Journey to the Western Isles of Scotland.* Dublin, 1775
Johnston, T.L., Buxton, N.K. & Mair, D. *Structure and Growth of the Scottish Economy.* London, 1971
Jones, R.M. 'Location of Industry and Distribution of Industry Policy in Great Britain', in Devine, P.J., Jones, R.M., Lee, N. & Tyson, W.J. *An Introduction to Industrial Economics.* London, 1974
Kellas, J.G. 'Highland Migration to Glasgow and the Origin of the Scottish Labour Movement', *Bulletin of the Society for the Study of Labour History,* Vol. 12, 1966
Kellas, J.G. *The Scottish Political System.* Cambridge, 1973
Knox, J. *A Tour Through the Highlands of Scotland and the Hebride Isles in 1786.* London, 1787
Lewis Association, *Reports 1–8.* Stornoway, 1945–53
The Lewisman, Stornoway
Littlejohn, J. *Westrigg: the sociology of a Cheviot parish.* London, 1963
Macdonald, Dr of Gisla. *Tales and Traditions of the Lews.* Stornoway, 1967
MacGregor, A.A. *Behold the Hebrides!* London, 1925
MacGregor, A.A. *The Haunted Isles, or Life in the Hebrides.* London, 1933
MacGregor, A.A. *The Western Isles.* London, 1949
Mackenzie, C. *Whisky Galore.* London, 1969
Mackenzie, W.C. *History of the Outer Hebrides.* Paisley, 1903
Mackenzie, W.C. *The Book of the Lews.* Paisley, 1919

Macleod, F. 'A Study of Gaelic-English Bilingualism: the effects of semantic satiation', Unpublished M.A. thesis, Aberdeen University, 1966

Macleod, F. 'An Experimental Investigation into some Problems of Bilingualism'. Unpublished Ph.D. thesis, University of Aberdeen, 1969

Mitchell, J. *Reminiscences of my life in the Highlands.* 2 vols., 1883. Facsimile edition, Newton Abbot, 1971

Moisley, H.A. 'The Deserted Hebrides', *Scottish Studies*, Vol. 10, 1966

Murray, W.H. *The Hebrides.* Heinemann, 1966

Napier Report. *Report of Her Majesty's Commissioners of Inquiry into the
Conditions of the Crofters and Cottars in the Highlands and Islands of
Scotland.* 1884

Nicolson, N. *Lord of the Isles: Lord Leverhulme in the Hebrides.* London,
1960

North 7 (Highlands and Islands Development Board), Issue No. 10, 1971

Our Changing Democracy. Cmnd 6348, H.M.S.O., 1975

Parman, S., 'Socio-cultural Change in a Scottish Crofting Township'. Unpublished Ph.D. thesis, Rice University, Texas, 1972

Patterson, I. 'The History of Education in Lewis'. Unpublished M.Ed.
thesis, University of Aberdeen, 1970

Pitt-Rivers, J. *People of the Sierra.* London, 1954

Rent Rolls. *Rent Rolls for the Lewis Estates, Barvas Parish (1851–1922).*
Stornoway Public Library

Review of Highland Policy. Cmnd 785, London, 1959

Rose, R. *The United Kingdom as a Multinational State.* Strathclyde University Survey Research Centre Occasional Paper No. 6, 1970

Rosenfeld, H. 'An overview and critique of the literature on rural politics',
in Antoun, R. & Harik, I. (eds.) *Rural Politics and Social Change in the
Middle East.* Bloomington, Ind., 1972

Royal Commission (Highlands and Islands) 1892, *Report and Minutes of
Evidence*, Vol. 2, Edinburgh, 1895

Scott, W. *Guy Mannering.* London (Everyman edition), 1974

Scott Report. *Report on Home Industries in the Highlands and Islands.*
1914

Scottish Economic Committee. *Review of the Economic Conditions with
Recommendations for Improvement.* 1938

Seebohm, F. *The English Village Community* (1883). Facsimile edition,
Port Washington, NY, 1971

Select Committee on Emigration. *First Report from the Select Committee
on Emigration. Scotland, together with minutes of Evidence and
Appendix.* 1841

Smith, W.A. *Lewsiana, or life in the Hebrides.* London, 1875

Smout, T.C. *A History of the Scottish People, 1560–1830.* London, 1969;
Fontana edition, 1972

Stacey, M. *Tradition and Change: a Study of Banbury.* Oxford, 1960

Stacey, M. 'The Myth of Community Studies', *British Journal of Sociology*,
Vol. 20, 1969

Stacey, M., Batstone, E., Bell, C. & Murcott, A. *Power, Persistence and
Change: a second study of Banbury.* London, 1975

Steel, T. *The Life and Death of St Kilda.* London (Fontana edition), 1975

Stornoway Gazette

Bibliography

Taylor Report. *Department of Agriculture for Scotland: Report of the Commission of Enquiry into Crofting Conditions.* 1954

Thompson, F. *Lewis and Harris.* Newton Abbot, 1960

Thompson, F. *Harris Tweed: the story of a Hebridean industry.* Newton Abbot, 1969

Thomson, D. *An Introduction to Gaelic Poetry.* London, 1974

Thomson, J. *The Value and Importance of the Scottish Fisheries.* Edinburgh, 1849

Tönnies, F. *Community and Association.* London, 1955

Vallee, F.G. 'Burial and Mourning Customs in a Hebridean Community', *Journal of the Royal Anthropological Institute*, Vol. 85, 1955

Walpole Report. *Report of the Commission Appointed to Inquire into Certain Matters Affecting the Interests of the Population of the Western Highlands and Islands of Scotland.* 1890

Webber, N. 'Lewis at Risk', *The Architect's Journal*, April, 1975

Weightman, G. 'Shadows on the Stones', *New Society*, 19 December 1974

The West Side Story, Shawbost School, 1964

Wolfe, B. *Scotland Lives.* Reprographia, Edinburgh, 1973

Youngson, A.J. *After the Forty-Five; the economic impact on the Scottish Highlands.* Edinburgh, 1973

Index